Introduction

Welcome. You're about to enter a world unlike any other. Here's a story that'll never be duplicated by anyone in the history of this planet. Have I overdone the introduction to this book? Probably. This is a story of a boy—wait a teenager—who lost an ability to survive the life of a teenager. This teenager buried himself inside of himself. He stayed away from everyone else and refused to accept who he had become. I hope with this book, the next version of himself can be better than him.

Does that sound compelling? I hope so. Look, writing is hard. I think attempting to write something is one of the toughest things a person can do. For me it's been the toughest thing I've had to accomplish in my life. And after you read my story, I think you'll be amazed by the fact I'm saying that. I hope I did a good enough job of writing this book, as I wrote this book with the thought of one select group of people to hear my words. I don't want to give any spoilers away by telling you who that group is.

This book is self-published. With some help from a great editor, I think we did a pretty good job. Sure, it doesn't have a major publishing house with a great ghostwriter next to it and opinions from people who have been writing all their lives. Read the acknowledgment section in any book. It's never just the author who completes a book. This book is just me and an editor. I just hope you enjoy this bit of self-published work, and we can grow the written word. Writing is a lost art, and I hope this book inspires you to write—even if you aren't in the select group that this book is meant for. Be a writer.

Finally, this book has a lot of references to random things. I'll give you an answer to the references by putting them in parenthesis at the end of each one. I'll explain the reason behind all of the references at the end of the book. No, no come on. let's read it now. (South Park)

1

I was in the third grade and my brother CJ, who was in the fifth grade, ran for class president at Booth Hill Elementary School. It was a simpler time in my life in more ways than one.

In elementary school we would have class elections every year, and the only students who could vote in those class elections were kids in the third, fourth, and fifth grade. Because of this it was a mortal lock for my brother to win the election as no other candidate had a sibling in the race for president. All I had to do was tell my friends that my brother was running for president and he wins. We had the numbers on our side. The non-existent pollsters couldn't mess this one up. I say that because the entire third grade knew me; thus, more people knew of my brother compared to the other candidates. The key to any good campaign is communication from every member of a campaign team. Buh. (The Dan Le Batard Show with Stugotz)

It was a weekday night and one of my mom's cousins, Gary, who was a very talented artist, came to our house to help my brother create posters for the election. The posters were meant to be taped to hallway walls around Booth Hill Elementary and entice the voting public to vote for my brother. The only thing that would've been better is to give every student a piece of butterscotch candy.

With the posters completed it became the responsibility of me, my brother and my mom to spend the night taping the posters all over our elementary school to help his election. My cousin went on to draw pictures of Pikachu, which kids were going crazy for back in 1999. He also drew a poster of Godzilla stepping on skyscrapers in New York City. The last poster was of Darth Vader with a caption saying, "I command you to vote for C.J. Metz for class president." All three posters were incredibly well done and seemed like work that could be hung in an art museum, much less an elementary school hallway. We did one walk-through and found the three areas that had the highest student population throughout the day. Believe it or not this was done without the need for scientific polling data. It was impossible for kids our age to not fall in love with those posters. As the election came, both my mother and brother told me to mention the fact that my brother is running for school president. I was told we need people to know that you two are related, because it'll swing the election his way.

I never spoke up to anyone about my brother running for president. Kids would go by his poster and say, "Hey, that's a pretty cool poster." I would look up at the poster knowing I saw who created it and who was mentioned on the poster but failed to say anything. My only action was to nod in agreement. It wasn't like I disliked my brother; I was just extremely shy. By third grade it was clear I wouldn't have a career as a campaign manager. To defend myself twenty-one years later, I assumed my friends were smart enough to see we had the same last name, and they knew to vote for the person with the same last name as me. Plus my friends had met my brother before. People don't give nine-year-old's enough credit when it comes to knowledge and understanding of politics #givenineyearoldstherighttovote.(Last Week Tonight with John Oliver) Was that too far?

My brother would end up winning the school election in what I assumed was a landslide. We didn't get to see the actual votes, and my brother was awarded the student presidency of Booth Hill Elementary School. I knew my classmates could do it.

As a kid my friends would ask me, "Who's your best friend?" It was one of those silly questions that kids have to worry about in elementary school. Because the only thing you really have to worry about in elementary school is friendship and what time recess starts.

Whenever I was asked that question, my response would always be that my brother is my best friend. Although a part of me was saying that so I didn't lose friendships with every new person who asked me that question in elementary school. What I was actually saying was 100- percent true; my brother truly was my best friend. Both of my parents were single children growing up, and as my brother and I grew up they would continually tell us about how they would be lonely as kids without a sibling in their houses. They both had wished they had brothers and sisters to talk with and play with during their days as children. My brother and I would take their words to heart as we did everything together as kids. We would play Nintendo 64 video games, play catch with a football or baseball, shoot hoops together, and watch sports whenever we had free time. I would go to my friends' houses and see them openly fight with their siblings right in front of me. They would yell to their parents that Billy was playing video games on the television we wanted to use. It was strange, as my brother and I were very different in that way.

C.J. graduated from elementary school and moved to the local middle school in sixth grade. Our bond started to lessen a little, as we were no longer students at the same school. We used to both exit the school bus together at the end of every school day and walk home at the same pace. We rarely had conversations on our walks; we both knew the comfort of us walking together was enough. Also we would never communicate the fact that we wanted to play Nintendo 64 when we got home; we would somehow just magically end up playing a game of Mario Kart after we threw our backpacks on the kitchen table. Those days were now gone as our time schedules would change with my best friend going to a new school.

My grades in elementary school were very average. The straight-C life was the life for me. It was the kind of report card your parents don't truly get angry about; they just shame you by saying "I'm disappointed, because I know you can do better." Which causes you to debate which is worse, failing by receiving a F and knowing you're at your worst, or receiving a C and knowing you're average. Because of my need to be average, I would have to race to the mailbox every quarter to prevent my parents from seeing my average report card. My plan was to always beat them to the mailbox and perform some type of David Blaine magic with the report card and cause my grades to change from C's to A's.

Academically I was an average student, but my spin zone (Pardon My Take) for my days at school was that I would always get an A in physical education. I say this because my mom was a physical education teacher. To all the kids and parents out there, it's physical education and not gym class. I wanted to get that message in writing as that was preached to me my entire life by my mom.

As a kid I loved being active, whether it was playing sports with my brother or being involved in Little League baseball and recreational basketball. Unfortunately, my above-average performance in physical education wouldn't allow me to get away with doing poor academically.

I reached into the mailbox and grabbed the envelope from Booth Hill Elementary School and carried it to my room without opening it. Why worry and bother to open it when you already know the grades? My worry was with what I was going to say my mom. My planned quote was "But mom, I tried my best, and I studied every single night I came home. I could've sworn my grades would've been better this quarter." I threw the envelope on my bed and let my brain continually create a quote that the world's greatest publicist would grow to envy.

As words and sentences continued to form in my head, I finally heard it—the garage door starting to open and a car pulling in. My mom being the only one who parked her car in the garage indicated that my time was up. All she had to do was walk from the garage to my bedroom door and then it was officially over. At that point I would have to quit stalling and tell her my marks.(Family Guy) A stopwatch would tell you it only takes a person ten seconds to walk from the garage to my bedroom door. On report card day my mom's time always seemed quicker.

Every school day my mom would ask, "How was your day today?" Every day after school my way of unwinding was either watching television or playing video games for an hour or two. I would never go straight to my desk and work on my homework. On report card day I would sit at my desk because I felt my average grades didn't give me the right to play video games or watch television. If I had that stance every night, then maybe my grades would've been better. The more you know.

 If I could eat the report card (Dan Le Batard Show with Stugotz) causing it to never be seen by anyone, I probably would have. But the report card needed to be signed by a parent, and my mom's caring curiosity about my day would always cause me to give in and hand it to her. Plus, I doubt report card paper tastes any good. In fact, it probably tastes worse than "regular paper" to prevent kids from eating their report cards. I think everything has to be digital by now anyway. What were we talking about again?

Realizing I shouldn't allow my mom to stand next to my door forever, I would never respond to hor question of 'How are you?' I would just take the walk of shame from my desk and hand her my report card. She took it with a disgruntled look knowing full well if I had to take it out of the mailbox myself, it probably wasn't a good report card. She stared at it for about five seconds and said, "Straight C's again, Cory?" This would cause me to go into my puppy dog-eyes phase and look up while saying, "I tried my best this quarter." She would always look back and say "I hope you did" while signing my card.

My grades were average but my brother, who was now in the sixth grade, was a certified genius. He came home with straight A's every quarter. It didn't matter what subject it was. I would sit at the kitchen table and hear about his great report card. We would both put in an equal amount of time for homework every school night. In fact, most nights I would actually put in more time, because school was tougher for me. Yet, he would get A's and I would get C's. As a kid I always wondered, 'how does it come so easy to him, and not me?' There would be nights he wouldn't even study at all, and he would still come home with A's. I didn't resent my brother for this; I just wished that it could've been me during some of my tough school days and nights.

Because my brother wasn't being challenged enough in school, he transferred to Hopkins School in New Haven, Connecticut, for his seventh-grade education (and what I had to assume would be beyond that). I knew I wasn't smart enough to get into Hopkins, and because of that I knew that we would never go to school together again.

As my fifth-grade education was wrapping up, I would finish my homework by 7:00 PM and go to my brother's room to ask, "Do you want to play video games?" I hated to see our N64 collect dust. For all of the N64 lifers out there, do you remember how you had to take the game out of the system and blow into the bottom of the cartridge for the game to work? Those were the days of using your lungs to get a video game to work. Something today's young whippersnappers will never understand. I'm starting to feel old already. Every night my brother would look at me and say, "I can't tonight, I'm still working on my homework." He's still working on homework? He never worked on his homework longer than me before.

To see my brother finally getting challenged in school and watching the work he was putting in gave me motivation to work just as hard as him. That's when my grades started to turn around and I left fifth grade with A's and B's on my report card, instead of straight C's.

Elementary school was now over, and it was time to move to Hillcrest Middle School. Going into middle school, the word 'nervous' wasn't in my vocabulary. Luckily, all of my friends from my elementary school would be coming with me to middle school, so there was no awkward get to know you phase, which was good. The only upsetting part of this new chapter in my life was the fact that I couldn't look forward to being in the same school as my brother.

I loved my time in middle school because I saw myself in every kid. What made me an all-around regular kid was that on one day, I could talk about and play sports with the athletic kids. And then the next day, I could talk about introvert things like television and video games with a different group of kids, as I enjoyed those things just as much. Because of that I enjoyed pretty much every day of my three years in middle school.

2

As important as friendship became for me during middle school, I knew I could always use more friends in life. Man's best friend became my new friend. One of my friends in middle school had recently gotten a pug. Earlier in my childhood my family had a Doberman, and I heard that she was a great dog. I didn't really have a memory of her as my family got her when I was a really young. So I didn't have moments in my life where I spent time with man's best friend. Every time I went over to my friend's house, his dog would greet me and wag her tail. She added to the fun of hanging out there, as we would play video games and play fetch with his dog.

Conversations about my friend's dog started to happen with my family, and we eventually started to think about owning a dog of our own. My mom came to pick me up one night and met my friend's dog. She asked my friend's mom where she found her dog. She told my mom the breeder's name and within a week we were in contact with her and scheduled an appointment to meet her at her house. She told us she only had one male puppy that we could come and visit.

It was a Saturday afternoon and my dad was on a business trip. The three of us didn't want to wait for him, as we were discussing and researching dog names the entire week. We came up with the name Rocky. We were 99% sure we would end up bringing Rocky home, yet there was doubt on whether we would fall in love with him.

All three of us walked into the breeder's house and there he was. A three-month-old puppy that immediately started wagging his tail and jumping into my mom's arms once she sat down. My mom picked him up and he started to bite and chew on her hair, as if he was biting down on his favorite chew toy. As all three of us looked at him, we knew we had a new pet in our family. And of course, we fell in love with him.

About a year after we got Rocky, mom was looking at his paws and noticed that he had dried blood on his front paws. He also seemed to have trouble walking any distance. Seeing this, she had to set Rocky up with an appointment with the veterinarian in our town.

All four of us this time went with Rocky to support our version of man's best friend. My mom carried him into the waiting room, as we feared what walking was doing to his little body with every step he took. Before walking toward the receptionist, my mom handed Rocky off to me. I held him in my arms, and I looked into his eyes wondering what he could be thinking. I knew my thoughts were silly because he's a dog. His only thoughts were running in an open field and eating food … having a life that's simple and easy. Which is something every living being deserves—a life that's simple and easy. What made his situation worse was that he was just a defenseless animal. It's not like he could speak up and say anything about his situation; he was just a living creature who enjoyed eating and playing with tennis balls. As my mom sat back down and I handed Rocky back, I could trust one true instinct: no dog deserves to have bloody paws or ever be in pain.

The veterinarian assistant entered the waiting room with a voice loud enough for Rocky to hear.
"Rocky!"

He turned his little head to the random person calling his name, and as he turned I started to see a wag in his curled-up tail. A greeting he would give to every new face he met without even knowing what they wanted. She led us to the examination room.

The vet entered the room with a smile and asked, "How are all of you?" He seemed to be in shock to see an entire family in the room for one appointment. I looked at his face and he started to lose his smile ever so slightly. I'm sure he realized that if an entire family comes in for an appointment, they must be very concerned.

My mom took charge as she's always done and told the vet about his bloody paws and his inability to walk long distance. The vet walked toward Rocky as he was still wagging his tail, living in a world where he didn't know what this man in a white lab coat was doing in front of him. The vet started to touch Rocky all over his body to see if he would react to anything. His only reaction was to continue to wag his tail and attempt to lick the vet's face. You know, dog stuff. After seeing Rocky having no reaction to touching him and seeing the dry blood on his paws, it was clear to the vet that something was going on. Looking at our concerned faces, he suggested an MRI for Rocky in the next week.

It's funny, the day my dad came home from his business trip he asked, "Who's going to take care of the dog?" My brother and I both said, "We would take care of him." My dad repeated, "Who's taking care of the dog?" He knew full well that my brother and I tended to tell white lies, as most teenagers do. That was his funny way of dismissing the idea that we would put the time in to take care of the dog. We both swore to him we would alternate taking Rocky for a walk whenever Rocky wanted to go for one. We assured our dad that Rocky is our responsibility. My dad rolled his eyes and greeted the dog with a smile.

Every morning 6:30 AM would come with Rocky's eyes opening, indicating it was time for a walk. My dad would walk over to both of our rooms and say, "Who's taking the dog out?" Eventually, my dad would stop waiting for us, and he would walk Rocky every morning, thus putting the responsibility on him. Because of this, my dad's relationship with Rocky was the strongest out of all four of us, so he took Rocky to get his MRI.

My brother and I were playing video games when all of the sudden my mom entered the room. I paused the game knowing if my mom needed to talk with us during video game time it was important.

She had one of those serious looks where you could've sworn one of us was in trouble. I thought back to what I did in the past 24 hours and couldn't think of anything bad. Could I have possibly forgot to make my bed? I looked toward my brother, and he didn't have a shred of guilt on his face.

My mom bent down and told us Rocky had a tumor on his spinal cord, and we'll have to take him in for surgery sometime over the summer. That was the first time anyone had ever delivered such bad news to me. I was only thirteen at the time. How much bad news could I have had? Life wasn't anywhere close to hitting me hard at the age of thirteen.

The dog all four of us grew to love over the past eight months already had issues at a young age. What will his future hold? Why did this have to happen to our innocent dog? What's a tumor? I had so many questions. The only answer I could think of is to say that life isn't fair.

▯

3

My grandparents bought a summer house in Lake George, New York, in 1997. With every summer I would look forward to the three-and-a-half-hour drive from my house in Connecticut. Whenever summer came around the previous ten months of struggling with school would disappear. It was now time to celebrate the season of summer. Not to be confused with the "Summer of George." (Seinfeld) Getting away and going on boat rides and swimming in Lake George always brought a smile to my face as a kid. To escape the world of books and school brought a feeling beyond belief.

It was the middle of the summer when Rocky's issues began, and our vet had suggested bringing Rocky to Tufts University for his surgery, as they had a very well-known veterinarian program. The four of us went up to Tufts and handed Rocky off to the complete strangers. You never think it's really that tough to leave your pet; you do it every time you walk out the door. This time was different because he wasn't staying in our warm loving home—he was staying at a strange place where they were going to operate on his little body. As we walked away from Rocky and went back to our normal lives, I thought about how it wasn't right. How do I get to live my normal life while he gets operated on? If only the roles were reversed.

The next day we all went back to Tufts to see the dog we loved. On the car ride there I started to think, would Rocky be any different after his surgery? Will this surgery cause him to be a different dog? Maybe that was a stupid and selfish question. But I knew deep down if anything like this ever happened to me things would change. How could they not? My final conclusion was to just make sure my friendship with him didn't change. No matter what happens, treat him like nothing has changed. No matter how he acts or looks, he's still the great dog we brought home eight months ago.

We went to the receptionist's desk and my mom quickly said, "Hi, we're here to check on Rocky." The receptionist went to the back where I assumed all of the pets were resting and told us, "He's resting in the back, do all of you want see him?" In that moment there was nothing I could want more in life than to see Rocky's wagging tail and his happy demeanor.

As we walked toward Rocky, we would see other dogs and I would be lying if I didn't say I was nervous. I saw dogs that were heavily sedated and wouldn't bother to look at you because they were so tired. They weren't the playful dogs you dream about coming home to after a long day of school or work.

All four of us walked together as we approached Rocky's cage in the hopes that if he saw us walking together it would lessen his pain and our pain.

We stood at the front of the cage. I took a quick glance. I didn't have a clear look at him, as I was still a couple of feet away. But I knew there was a small dog in the shape of a pug in the back of that cage. The vet tech opened the cage, and with the trepidation of a child walking into his first day of kindergarten, Rocky looked up at us with the same puppy eyes we fell in love with the day we got him.

Unfortunately, this time his entire back was painted fire engine red, covered with a number of staples I couldn't even count. Rocky kept staring at the ground, looking like he was cowering in fear of what would happen to him next. My mom gently said, "Rocky." He looked up and started to wag his tail, realizing who we were and trying to greet us like he always did. Seeing this, my mom immediately told us to bend down to his level. We bent down into a catcher's stance to greet him. I played catcher a couple of times as a kid so I understood the stance when I was staring at a pitcher in front of me, but it was very foreign when looking at my dog. It was even more foreign in the sense that I was used to him jumping on my legs and running around me. My reaction to his running would always be to grab his toys, as he would run around the family room like the Energizer Bunny. This happened like clockwork every day I came home.

Once my eyes were set on Rocky, he attempted to walk my way. I went toward him and almost made the mistake of petting his entire back and putting my hand over his red dye and staples. It was such a common greeting that we had every day; the red dye and staples along his back never crossed my mind.

I didn't say anything or do anything. I had to just stare, because I didn't know what else to do. This wasn't the dog I knew. We carried him to his crate, as he wasn't ready to be put on a leash yet, and we brought him home. By the end of the summer with a little rest and healthy eating, Rocky was back to his old self. I couldn't have been prouder of him.

The last weekend of the summer came around, and I took one final jump from our dock into beautiful Lake George. Lake George was the kind of lake you would want to purify yourself in after a game of basketball.(Chappelle's Show) Swimming from the dock to the beach with every stroke of my arms and kick of my legs felt like any normal summer. At this point in the story it was my sixth season at Lake George, and it was finally coming to an end. A new school year was about to begin.

My mom was sitting on the beach when she looked at me and strangely said, "Cory, come over here." I looked back at her with strange curiosity, wondering what that tone of voice meant. It wasn't an angry tone, so I knew I wasn't in trouble. I would describe it as a scared tone. I was literally five feet away, and now I was being told to walk closer. I stepped toward my mother and looked at her face, expecting her to give me some kind of news. She looked at me and said nothing as I turned back toward our house. She spun my body around, causing me to face the lake that I have enjoyed my entire life. She was staring directly at the center of my back, and she started to trace her finger up and down my spine.

I don't know if it was the bright sun or that my mom wanted to deliver the news in a different setting. I was told to walk up the road and back to the beach house. As we walked back, I didn't say anything to my mother. What's there to discuss when you have no idea what is happening?

My mom asked me to stand in the middle of the family room and look out the door. No argument came from me, as I looked out the door and saw Lake George—the childhood paradise I always loved.

I was told to raise my arms outward and touch my toes like some sort of contortionist. As I accomplished this very complicated move, I started to realize this probably wouldn't be an accomplishment to be proud of. I reached down as far as I could and without the distraction of the sun, my mom told me we have to schedule a visit with an orthopedist. I looked back at her and asked, "Why? "You have a case of scoliosis. I can clearly see it by the shape of your spine. An orthopedist will be able to evaluate you and tell you the next thing we need to do for you." What could be next?

4

The day finally came for an appointment with the orthopedic doctor at Yale-New Haven Hospital. I had to miss a day of school. At this point, missing a day of school hurt me the most, because I didn't like the feeling of being behind others. The idea of catching up while I lagged behind always upset me for some reason. I guess I just didn't like knowing that I missed out on the same opportunity that others had. It's why I had perfect attendance in seventh grade.

My mom drove me to the hospital but we didn't talk on our way there. There wasn't much to say, as I really didn't even know what scoliosis was. This was a time before smartphones and the need to be encompassed in your phone every second. There was an opportunity for a discussion, but I just didn't want to have it.

Exiting the parking garage and walking in did cause a little stress, as I had never entered a hospital before. Before we check in with the receptionist, my mom looked at my face and could sense I had a 'deer in the headlights' look and didn't want to speak up. My mom came to the rescue, which wouldn't be the first time and said, "Hi my son, Cory Metz, has an appointment with Dr. Renshaw." The receptionist looked up at me and said, "Ah, Cory Metz, you're a new patient here, I'll need you and your mom to fill out a few pages of paperwork if you don't mind." I smiled and said "Sure." She replied, "And before you do that please tell me your birthday." I told her my birthday and grabbed the paperwork as my mom and I went down the list, not minding too much as this will probably be the last time I fill out paperwork at Yale-New Haven Hospital.

"Cory Metz." I looked around as if it was the first time that I had ever heard my name and walked toward the voice. In the examination room, thoughts about the possibilities of what this ordeal could mean didn't enter my mind. There's nothing to stress out about here, I'm just here for a quick visit.

I plopped myself onto the examination table and looking at my mother while we were waiting for the doctor, we again said nothing to each other. It was clear we both couldn't understand what this moment could mean for my future so discussing it didn't have any value.

The doctor walked in, said hello to the both of us, and stared at my chart. Looking at him, I was just hoping to not get marked as a difficult patient on his chart! (Seinfeld) Although I didn't think I'd ever see Dr. Renshaw again, that would be devastating to my fragile ego.

"We'll have to bring you to the next room for an X-ray." As a kid, I wasn't a risk taker and never had an X-ray; I didn't even know what it was for. But, I watched my fair share of cartoons and saw cartoon versions of X-ray's. The Grinch being the most popular X-ray image when his heart grows three sizes that day. I mean, animation and real life are very similar, right? Who hasn't had an anvil fall on them? Before getting the X-ray, I looked at the doctor and thought about asking him if real X-rays are like cartoon X-rays. Luckily, I maintained my dignity and didn't ask.

Entering the room, I spotted a large rectangular blackboard on a pole. There was no chalk or eraser in the room, so the math class I had missed that day couldn't be taught on this board. The X-ray technician looked at this healthy teenager who had come into his room and asked, "How are you?" I looked back at him and said, "I'm good." It wasn't manufactured sincerity. I was actually good at that moment.

 The technician pointed and told me to walk toward the blackboard and press my nose against the X-ray board. As I pressed my nose against the board, I officially knew this wasn't anything like a math class.

The next request was to twist and turn my body and face to the right while holding my arms out. I was starting to wonder if the next command was going to be to attempt the Macarena. Remember the Macarena? It was fantastic.(South Park) My body was finally done—turn, turn, turn there is a season (Turn, Turn, Turn, by The Byrds)—and I was brought back to my examination room.

I wasn't really nervous, because I didn't know what these results could mean in the grand scheme of my life. My mom already told me my spine was curved and that she knew there was something wrong with me, and a X-ray only further proved that fact. I just wanted to know what the doctor could do about this. I just wanted to get back to being a normal teenager. Dealing with doctors has already gotten old, and this was my first-ever visit to a doctor outside of my dentist and pediatrician. For a split second, I thought about yelling to anyone who was willing to listen. "Why me?" I tried to do everything right in life. I wasn't a bully in school; why do I have to be here? I always tried to be a good person. I'm here and Michael Bay gets to keep making movies. (South Park) Just let me leave.

The doctor walked in once again and put my X-ray on the light-up board in the corner and put us in the dark. There it was: a spine in the shape of a question mark. When you see your spine in the shape of a question mark it forces you to ask questions. How did this happen? Why did this happen? When did this happen? So many questions I wanted to have answered.

The doctor grabbed a pencil, a compass, and a protractor and then went to work. He started to trace along my spine as if he was in kindergarten completing one of his assignments for his teacher. There was a part of me that had to laugh as something as silly as tracing; a skill you learned in pre-school is deciding my life.

He finished his art project and looked directly at my mother and me. "Well, you were right to come here, as Cory does have a case of scoliosis." Looking at him I thought my mom had already told me I had scoliosis, and I trusted her opinion to be correct. That wasn't the news I wanted to hear … please give me something new.

As he studied his artwork one more time, he turned to me and said, "if you look at your spine, Cory, you'll see your spine curves to the left. Typically, scoliosis curves to the right. Now because of this we'll have to schedule an MRI. I'm not saying there's something wrong with you, but because your curve is going the opposite way of typical scoliosis, there may be something on your spine." Something on my spine, what could that mean? Something like a speck of dirt seeped through my skin? My spine doesn't show dirt!(Family Guy) I knew that because I always tried to keep my back clean in the shower. Were there nights I may have missed a spot and didn't clean my entire back? It's a possibility. We all make mistakes sometimes.

I didn't ask any questions and just let my mom schedule the M.R.I at the front desk. I just wanted to go home and be a normal teenager who comes home from school, does some schoolwork, then watches some television and plays video games. I repeat this process every weekday until it's time to hang out with friends on the weekend. It will be nice when my life is like that once again.

The day of the M.R.I came. It was scheduled for 4:45 PM on a school day. I still made the trip to school that day and refused to tell my friends about what I was doing that afternoon. It wasn't the kind of thing where you stop a friend in a hallway and brag. Hey guess what? It's three letters and I have no idea what it entails. MRI.

I honestly didn't care too much about the MRI because just like the previous doctor's visit, and the first discovery of my spine being curved, I had no point of reference. If I had asked the doctor what this MRI test means for my future, he may have replied, "It could mean everything."

Maybe I would've told some of my friends about the test. Instead, I looked at this MRI as just as a silly exam that will end up proving nothing, and I can move on with my life. I know I will be back to spending time with good friends and silly middle school things like going to dances and just hanging out with friends. The life you dream about in elementary school.

I got home from school that day, and my mom was already standing by the door ready to take me back to Yale New-Haven Hospital. She left work early to prevent me from being late to the appointment. She told me to change out of my school clothes so we could leave. Changing clothes became an afterthought in that moment as I didn't know what was proper to wear to your first MRI, and I didn't really care to know. I still held the belief that visiting Yale-New Haven Hospital wouldn't be a reoccurring thing for me, and I was already wearing fairly presentable jeans with a long-sleeve shirt. My mom gave me one look knowing I didn't change and chose not to argue with my wardrobe and not wanting to change out of my school clothes and said, "Let's go."

As the adult in this situation, it was clear my mom knew what this all could mean and turned the car radio down a little at the start of the trip and waited for me to open up. We sat in silence for the first ten minutes, as I wasn't in the mood to strike up a conversation. Tired of the silence, my mom turned down the radio even more—though it was already turned down pretty low—and asked, "Do you know what an MRI is?" I looked at her and said, "No."

"I've had one." In that moment I wasn't really in the mood for a pep talk. But I knew my mom was just trying to do the right thing by telling me I'll be okay. So I turned to listen to what she had to say. She went on to tell me she had one on her knee and that it shouldn't take too long. "It's just a long series of beeping noises. Nothing will come out and scare you; all you'll have to do is just lie down flat and stay perfectly still," she said. "Eventually someone will come in and tell you the test is over, and you can go home. It'll be nice and easy."

We entered the hospital through a different entrance this time, and we had to walk to an entirely different area to find where the MRI machines were hidden. This was starting to get to a point where Yale could hire me as their new tour guide, which is exactly the thing I was attempting to avoid. "Good afternoon ladies and germs; that's an old hospital pun. Anyhow, now if you look to my left, you'll see a fountain where water shoots out. How am I doing so far?" Do tour guides randomly ask how they're doing in the middle of giving a tour? Hopefully you view that as the worst joke in this book. If you don't, then we're in trouble.

The MRI machines were kept in the basement of Yale-New Haven hospital. I assumed they kept the machines in the basement for good reason as they were incredibly loud. I started to hear the buzzing of the machines from a good fifty yards away. Imagine the sounds you've heard in every kids' cartoon you've ever watched. Those sounds were the sounds ringing through the hallway as we kept walking forward toward the noise. I would've preferred to turn back and walk the opposite way. But we both knew in order to move on with my life, I had to keep going and embrace what this meant for my future. There was no turning back now.

We took a seat in the mock waiting room, which was just four chairs along a wall outside the loud noises and waited for something to happen. There was no receptionist or anything like that. We started to wonder if we were in the right place and as soon as I thought about saying something (well really, my mom thought about saying something), a person came from behind the door and asked, "Are you the 4:45?" I thought about saying, yes, and if you could refer to me as the 4:45 for as long as I am here, instead of my proper name, that will really lighten the mood. The time for jokes ceased to exist, as my sarcastic side didn't feel like talking at that moment. My mom and I both replied, "Yes." He looked at us and said it'll be a few more minutes and then I'll be back. We both thanked him, and he went back behind the door.

The cartoon noises eventually stopped, and a grown man came out from behind the curtain looking kind of woozy. For the kids reading this book, it was the look you have when you walk from your bed to your bathroom mirror first thing in the morning. It didn't remind of anything else that you can legally do over the age of twenty-one. Kids book. (Barstool Sports Pizza Review) I looked at my mom and asked, "Will I look like that?" She just shrugged her shoulders. If my mom doesn't know what the future holds, then no one does.

The man behind the curtain came back and handed me some paperwork and asked, "Does your mother want to come back with you?" She immediately said, "Yes." That did bring me some sense of security as I was now becoming a petrified thirteen-year-old.

The paperwork was done, and it was time for my showdown with the machine. The MRI technician told me to take everything off except my underwear and put a blue smock on. As I held the smock, I thought about how I was reduced to this —spending a weekday night wearing an ugly smock that I wouldn't wear to an elementary school art class. If I could have found an emergency exit and had the ability to run back to the day before my mom noticed my spine was curved, I would have.

Walking out of the changing room my mom stood there and asked, "Are you ready to go?" Without any words I just shrugged my shoulders.

The MRI technician came out from behind the door for a final time and told me to follow him. A small part of me knew this journey was just beginning, although I didn't want to admit it.

Taking steps toward the tube wasn't as bad as I thought it would be. This tube didn't look scary at all. It kind of reminded me of Space Mountain at Walt Disney World. You know how at the beginning of the ride when the chain is carrying your train to the top, and it seems like you're in a tube and then the ride starts? The machine was still making noises as I walked closer, just like the noises you hear on Space Mountain. I started to think maybe this would be fun.

"Cory, I am going to need you to lie down as if you're about to take a nap." Hearing that I thought I would be allowed to take a nice nap; how bad can this MRI be? My mom stood next to me as I was lying on the machine and didn't say a word. I don't know if it was because she knew I wouldn't have anything to say if she attempted to talk with me, or she couldn't handle a conversation with her son when she knew this machine held the answers to his future.

My body slid into the machine and the cartoon noises started to ring in my head. I had to thank the technician for giving me earplugs, because the noises started to upset me pretty quickly. Buzz, bop, really any stupid sound you could think of, I ended up hearing it. It reminded me of the game Bop It, a silly game I used to play in the 90's. Getting an MRI is like a game of Bop It, but instead of twisting, pulling, and bopping the toy, you're lying perfectly still in a giant tube. Has any of this become fun, yet? If you bring Bop It to a book signing of mine, I'll be sure to sign it and beat you in a game. Just be sure to be last person in line out of respect of the other autograph seekers.

An hour passes, and the noises still ring around me. In that moment I thought, Would it have been weird if I just randomly yelled Bop It to no one? Sinking my eyeballs as low as I possibly could while not allowing my eyes to fall out of their sockets, I still saw my mom still standing there waiting for the test to end.

As the test continued into hour two, I started to get agitated. As a person who can handle being alone with his thoughts occasionally, enjoying two-hours lying down alone with my thoughts should have been an enjoyable experience. The thought of two hours to myself where no one bothered me, and I was alone with my thoughts, usually was my idea of heaven. The problem is that it's not enjoyable when you have to stay still for two hours and loud noises keep ringing in your ears. Being alone is fun when you can take a break from lying down and stretch every so often. Because of me wanting to move, I started to squirm as if I was playing a game of night crawlers.(It's Always Sunny in Philadelphia) The MRI tech told me before the start of the test that he needed me to remain still. My mom touched my foot, indicating that I needed to stop moving. I knew I was ruining the test, but I could no longer hold my body in a still position.

Next came a call on the speaker inside the machine, as if the principal was calling me for detention. He told me, "I know you've been here for a while Cory, and I know this is tough, but we need you to stop moving. We can't complete the test, if you continue to move." That's easy for him to say as he sits in a comfortable chair with the ability to move his back up and down, while I lie stiff as a board on a plastic table. I felt like I had a right to move at this point.

During my mental breakdown in the MRI machine, the technician did reassure me that the test would be over soon. I took some sense of pride in that and assumed he wasn't lying to me, so I tried to maintain stiff as a board. The minutes started to rack up, and it became three hours in the machine.

Once it hit three hours, I broke down a little in the machine. I twisted my entire body like a pretzel and didn't care what the repercussions were for messing up this stupid test. I wanted to yell, "You can use what you have." The technician once again came on the speaker. This time in a calming voice he asked, "Are you done, Cory?" Am I done? I was done two hours ago! I replied in the nicest way possible, "Yes, please." The tech said, "That's fine, let me get one more set in and I'll take you out." I took in one more breath of relief and stayed as stiff as I could for one more set, and I was brought out of the machine and back into civilization.

Mom asked, "Are you okay?" Looking up at her I didn't know how to react. Do I cry? No kids my age don't cry. I was just glad it was over and chose to say nothing. I walked back to change my clothes and looked forward to going home.

Mom got the phone call the next day about the MRI results. Again, I was playing video games. She told me to hit pause. With a serious face she said, "Cory, the MRI results weren't good, as you may have suspected based off of how long we were there. You'll have to get an appointment with a new doctor."

I now realized that this is serious. Before, I was just a teenager with a misshapen spine who got an MRI. Now because those results were not good, I have to meet with a different doctor. How many doctors will I have to meet with?

The morning of my appointment with the new doctor came, and my dad knocked on my door indicating it was time to wake up. In a relaxing voice he said, "Are you getting ready to go?" I looked at him and asked, "You're coming too?"

My dad coming to my appointment with us actually ended up reducing my fear somewhat. I always viewed my dad as my comic relief. If you ever needed a good laugh during a stressful time or even a painful time, my dad would come in with a funny story that would help diffuse the situation. He would make me realize that you just have to laugh sometimes.

The newest doctor on my now-growing list of doctors was named Dr. Duncan. He specialized in whatever was wrong with me, which I still had no idea what that was exactly. Sitting in the waiting room with my parents, I wanted to leave once again. I know some kids dream about being away from school and having days off, but I liked school. I liked the idea of having a social circle at school every day. I liked to learn new things in all of my classes.

After checking in with the reception, we went to meet with Dr. Duncan. There he was sitting behind his desk. Dr. Duncan was a man who could play any television grandpa you could think of. As he got up from his chair, a very tall man, I want to say around 6 feet tall, which was tall on my scale, came to shake the hand of all three of us. This was my first handshake with an adult that my parents didn't know. With that shake of a hand was I now officially an adult? What a feeling. But I didn't want to think about being an adult; I just wanted to know why I was here. Just give me some answers.

The three of us sat and stared with great anticipation waiting for him to say something of substance.

He looked directly at me and said, "Do you want to wait in the waiting room? This can be a tough thing to hear at your age, and if you don't want to be in this discussion, you're free to leave." I looked him in the eyes and said, "It's fine." Whether I heard it from him or not, either way this appointment was happening. I would rather hear it straight from the source instead of hearing it later from my parents. The doctor logged into his computer and showed us the MRI results.

I stared at the screen as if I was playing the greatest video game of all time. There it was on display, my curved spinal cord with strange marks on it. As I studied the screen, Dr. Duncan started talking. I hadn't paid any attention to what he was saying medically; I was just staring at the marks. The marks started to move up and down as Dr. Duncan started to click his mouse to indicate where the marks were on my actual spine. Eventually my eyes moved away and I heard Dr. Duncan say one thing: "Cory has tumor cells on his spine, and we will need to schedule surgery to remove the cells." Which he could have said from the beginning instead of giving me the laser light show of cells moving throughout my body. Although he probably did, and I just wasn't paying attention. It's those darn screens that always suck you in.

I waited to hear what our second option was. Instead, Dr. Duncan continued to stare directly at my parents, thus indicating a second option wasn't coming. But there's always a second option, right? I was hoping my mom or dad would eventually say there was. I wanted a second option that would allow me to escape this hospital with my old life back. I turned to both of my parents and waited for them to say something. My dad put it as simply as he could and replied, "Okay." My mom did the same by nodding her head in agreement.

I thought about dropping my jaw or walking out of the room in an upset mood, but what would that have accomplished? We came to Dr. Duncan for a reason. Based on of all the degrees hanging on the walls in his office, plus his years of experience, he must know what he's talking about. Who am I to throw a fit and tell this man he's wrong. The man is a doctor and he's only trying to do what's best for me. Please tell me the date and time, and I will be ready for surgery.

5

The week began with my surgery scheduled for the Friday following my appointment with Dr. Duncan. I could've gone to school all week and played the sympathy card with all of my friends. I decided not to and didn't mention the surgery to anyone. I played it off as if it was a routine surgery, like a kid getting his tonsils removed. My teachers were informed of my situation, and every single one pulled me out of class and told me not to stress about homework. They all said they'd make every effort to adjust for me when I come back. I thanked every teacher as their words held value, but it was the act of one teacher in particular who really helped me before my surgery.

About a month earlier, our Home Economics teacher gave us a booklet with pages and pages of things we could sew and bring home with us. I looked through the booklet and spotted stuffed footballs with college logos. I showed the booklet to my brother and asked, "Which one do you think I should pick?"

He replied, "You should pick Georgia. Their logo is pretty cool, and they have a pretty cool mascot, too." Always listening to his opinion, I decided to order the Georgia football.

The planned date to finish sewing happened to be the date of my surgery. I honestly didn't care that much about sewing a stupid football. I figured this would be the start of missing a few things in school. It's just a silly stuffed football. I have a few stuffed footballs from when I was a kid. I am sure this one isn't any different. My home economics teacher kindly allowed me to skip the assignments she had assigned for the rest of the class that day and allowed me to work on my stuffed football.

Both my mom and grandma knew how to use sewing kits. I could've paid attention to them and mastered the art of sewing. Instead, I always took the easy way out and handed anything that needed sewing straight to either willing participant and walked away. Why bother to learn something when someone else can do it for you?

The black-and-red fabric of the Georgia Bulldogs team colors sat on the table, and the do-it-yourself hat that I had never worn in my life was now on. Placing pins into the fabric, I started to think this whole sewing thing isn't so hard. Maybe I can create this stuffed football and turn this into a career. It seems simple enough.

Carrying my pieces of fabric over to the sewing machine and methodically stitching it together was the most challenging part, but with a little time and patience, the football was assembled. It turns out with a little instruction and a little can-do attitude, anything can be accomplished.

The final touch was stitching the letter G on the football. The letter G can represent a few words. Words like good and great. For me looking at the letter G stood for one word. Gee. As in gee, why me? Or just telling someone who was willing to listen, gee, I don't want any of this to happen.

Holding my completed football, I thought about variations of the word 'complete.' A word that hadn't crossed my mind. Until now. That word caused me to wonder about where I stand when it comes to completion of many things in my life. How will I complete the eighth grade now that I'll have to leave in the middle of it? Will my life completely change after this surgery? The number of variables in my life at the age of thirteen were beginning to add up.

The day before my surgery my alarm rang, and I refused to get out of bed. I began to act my age. I felt if I refused to leave my bed maybe this would all go away. The tumor cells will pack their bags and leave my body. My hope was they would leave and end up in a trash can for no one to ever see again. No one deserves the diagnosis I received from my doctor.

My mom came to my bedroom and saw how stubborn I was being. She took one look at me and said, "It's fine if you want to take the day off because of what's happening tomorrow, but you can't stay here all day. You have to come to work with me." I lifted my head out of my pillows and said, "That's fine." She looked at me in shock and said, "Okay, you'll have to get ready now." She was surprised with good reason. I could've gone to school and played up the fact that I was going in for surgery tomorrow. I could've received sympathy points from every single person in the school. I could've been the kid that had every face talking to me and wishing me good luck. Every single boy and girl could've shaken my hand or given me a hug. It could've been an incredibly memorable day with friends as I said my last goodbyes for who knows how long to everyone I knew. Instead, I shielded away from that and told my mom I'd go to her school and see kids I didn't even know. Although I liked school, if the day was going to become a sympathy show for me, I didn't want any part of it.

When I was younger, I would go to mom's middle school whenever I had snow days or random days off that her school district didn't have, and I would enjoy a day at Fairfield Woods Middle School. With gym being my favorite subject, walking into her school gymnasium when no kids were around was my version of a kid walking into a candy store.

Every time I walked into that gym, I would grab a basketball in the storage room and wait till it was a free period or a lunch period. That way no students were around, and I would shoot hoops by myself. I don't know what it was exactly about playing basketball alone that made it so appealing. I would say you're never alone when you shoot hoops by yourself. You do have someone else with you, or should I say you do have something with you when you shoot hoop alone. That something is the basketball. You have a friend in the orange circle that weighs twenty-two ounces.

Anyway, back to now. Dribbling the ball while walking into the gymnasium as if I was warming up in Madison Square Garden just felt right. Sure, I could've been getting sympathy from everyone at school today. Instead, all I did was focus on one thing. Taking two dribbles and shooting the ball. This process continued from every angle. As I ran around the court hearing the basketball clank off the rim after a shot or hearing a swish through the net, I never thought about what tomorrow would mean to me. Will my back hurt the next day? Will my life be the same after this surgery? Instead, I just kept my mind and eyes on the inflated orange circle moving in front of me.

As my mom drove me home, she saw this whole surgery thing was starting to deflate me, as I stared at the floor mats the entire trip. I didn't want her to attempt a conversation about anything in that moment. She looked at me and to brighten my day she said, "How about we go to the Trumbull Mall? You can go to any store in the mall and within a reasonable price range, you can have anything you want and bring it with you to the hospital." I looked up and thought, anything I want? I picked my head up and smiled, thinking that any small item in the mall could be some kind of savoir from the depression I was experiencing. We went to one store and one store only—Lids—where I spotted a Georgia Bulldogs hat. This hat was different from the football I had sewn together, because the hat had the face of a Bulldog on it. It's funny because I was never a big fan of wearing hats. I always thought they were kind of rude. When you wear a hat, it blocks the top of your head, thus not allowing the person you're talking with to see all of you. In a way, wearing a hat is a form of invisibility as it keeps you hidden from others. After everything I just went through over the past few weeks, I wanted that invisibility.

6

 The alarm rang at 5:30 AM, but I chose to ignore it. Hearing the sudden buzz of the alarm caused my body to jump up and head straight to the bathroom every morning on a school day. This time I didn't have that same sensation of jumping up; instead, I buried my head into my pillow. My hope was if I never left my bed this day would never happen. Maybe my tumor cells had magically disappeared from my spine overnight, and the pain that would become my life would never occur. I know that didn't work yesterday, but it never hurts to try to want something again.

Instead, my mom knocked on the door and said, "It's time to wake up, Cory." Hearing those words out loud forced me to finally come to realization that this surgery is happening. The decision was no longer mine, and I had to give in. My fate was so longer in my hands.

I performed the same routine I had done every single school morning, which involved me walking straight to the freezer and attempting to toast a waffle. This wasn't the brightest moment of my life, as I forgot that I couldn't eat anything on surgery day. My mom immediately ran over to the toaster and unplugged it. "What are you doing, Cory? You know you can't eat today!" I hoped the worst part of this day would be my inability to eat before surgery, and I threw my waffles into the garbage can.

My mom and dad drove me to Yale for "Surgery Day." A holiday that should never be celebrated. I spent the car ride staring out the window thinking about school. I thought about all the missing assignments in Math, Science, Spanish and English class. The amount of homework I'll have when I go back to school. How many days will I miss? Also, how will I ever get around to completing all of the schoolwork I will miss?

Arriving at Yale-New Haven Hospital for the fourth time had a different feel because this was the first time something was set in stone. The other three times I had visited the hospital my fate was still being discussed, and I didn't truly know what my final outcome would be. This time I had a solid idea of what this morning meant. I just didn't want to believe it.

All three of us walked in together as the tight knit group that we've been during these trying times and stood in front of the receptionist. I said nothing and my mom spoke up and stated my name. "Hello, Cory Metz." I hadn't matured enough to say my own name.

"Ah yeah, Cory, please take a seat, and we will bring you back when they're ready." When they're ready? I've never been ready, and I never will be ready. So, doesn't that cancel out the surgeon's ability to be ready. Which would mean I could leave.

Looking right at her, I just chose to walk the other way. Sometimes you just have to walk away in life. That was my final form of major protest by not uttering a word.

The chair in the waiting room didn't have a feel. The temperature in the waiting room didn't have a feel. The words coming out of the mouths of the patients and families in the crowded waiting room didn't make a noise—at least in my mind.

"Cory Metz?" I lifted my head looking for a different Cory Metz. I lifted my body in the slowest possible motion and walked toward the woman who called my name. She looked at me and put her hand out. I secretly was hoping she would say, "Oh Cory, it turns out we've been wrong about your results this entire time. You are perfectly healthy, and we were reading your file wrong this entire time. Please go home and accept this lollipop as an apology." Instead, she looked at me and said, "I'm sorry but we need you to remove your glasses as you're going in for your procedure now." I looked up and nodded with a blank stare at no one in particular. I turned around and looked at my parents, and it finally happened.

I broke down and started crying. This entire time I tried to act tough. Sure, I had moments where I was clearly upset by this, but I never cried. I wanted everyone to think I was an adult and that I was above all of this. In actuality, I was just a thirteen-year-old kid.

I cried as I walked back to my parents and handed my glasses to my mom. Neither one of us uttered a word. I think we both knew my tears said it all.

I walked to the back with tears streaming down my face, as I attempted to control myself as best I could. I was pointed into a waiting room and told to sit, change, and wait to be called into the surgery room.

As I changed into the hospital gown, I started to get my sense of feeling back. Although there wasn't a wind gust in the waiting room, my body started to feel cold. Maybe it was the openness of the hospital gown or the coldness that comes with being alone with your thoughts. I grabbed the gown and continued to shake my body, as if causing friction by shaking it would warm the coldness that I was feeling inside of my body.

Ten seconds into my shaking dance, a knock on the door came. "Hello, Cory, I am your anesthesiologist for your procedure. It's nice to meet you. It's my job to guide you through your surgery, today." I looked at her and shook her hand. "Have you ever had surgery, before?" With a smile I said, "No." I thought about saying, 'No, did you know I had perfect attendance last year?' I maintained my sense of vanity and didn't tell her as I knew it wouldn't matter in that moment. She told me about the surgery and what it will be like while I'm asleep. There were so many medical terms and things I didn't understand. I just continually shook my head up and down like a bobblehead doll. As soon as all of her medical jargon ended, she told me one final thing. "The anesthesia we give you can have a distinct smell. Would you like to choose a smell?"

As silly as this may sound, that was the first time that I was happy throughout this entire process. I say that because this was the first time I could make my own decision about something. My words can actually do something. There was never a point where I could say stop this three-hour MRI now. Or reschedule the date of this surgery to never. When it came to picking a smell, I was the decider. (American Dad)

As the list of smells went on, only one sounded good. Green apple. I loved green apple, because it was my favorite Jolly Rancher flavor. I believed I could still have my sense of being a kid if I had the smell of green apple going through my nose while I was about to go under the knife.

With a smile on my face I said, "Green apple, please!" She smiled back, as I imagined she hated to see kids come into surgery with a frown on their face. She put the clipboard down and asked one final question, "Are you ready?" Am I ready? It's a question I couldn't truly answer, as I didn't understand what I was getting ready for. If you asked me before a written test, "Are you ready?" my response would be," Yes I am ready." I could answer that question with some certainty, because I had studied the previous night. If you asked me if I was ready before I played a basketball game, I could say yes. I was practicing in the gym all week, and I studied the plays we were planning to run. Going into this surgery, I had no way of preparing myself for something that I had no possible way of understanding. I just took a deep breath and walked into the operating room.

The tears still hadn't disappeared off of my face completely. If the anesthesiologist offered her hand to me, I probably would've taken it. At this point my body started to ache and the surgery hadn't even started.

The door opened and the lights inside the operating room were blinding. Lights were everywhere! My eyes were drawn toward one particular light. It was the light sitting over a metal table. I had never seen a brighter light in my entire life. I thought about asking how many watts were in that light. Stupid question aside, I did take comfort in the fact the lights were very bright in hopes they'd be able to see the tumor and pull it off my spine.

Walking toward the metal table in the operating room, I started to replay what got me here. The day my mom told me to bend down and noticed my spine was curved. The day I went to Yale and the doctor told me I had scoliosis. The day I had my three-hour MRI. The day I was told I had tumors on my spine. And now I will be lying on this table right in front of me.

I climbed up onto the operating table. Lying on my back, I stared into the blinding bright light and closed my eyes. I thought if I stared directly into this light any longer, I would surely go blind. The anesthesiologist tapped my shoulder and said, "Take one more breath before I put the mask over your face."

The mask went on, and she started to count down. As soon as I heard ten, I thought about removing the mask and telling her to please give me more time. Nine. Wow, that gas really does smell like green apple. Eight. The anesthesiologist starts to touch my shoulder in hopes of comforting me. She told me to try to rest my eyes. Seven. My eyes were now closed. That's the last number I heard.

7

They call it knockout gas for a reason. All I heard was the sound of
the heart rate monitor beeping next to my still body. I looked down
at my hand as an IV drip was coursing through my veins. Staring at
my hand with the eyes of an eagle I knew this was no longer going
to be a walk in the park.

After waking up one thought came to mind: how about I go for a
walk? My body was lying comatose for the last few hours.
Walking was such a simple process, as it was something I had done
every morning after I took my first steps as a child. There's nothing
to it. I lifted my right leg up, and that was fine. I attempted to move
my left leg and that leg refused to cooperate with the right. Finally
gaining a sense of my surroundings I turned and saw my parents
sitting next to me.

I pleaded, "My leg isn't moving." Both of my parents jumped up together and quickly removed the blanket that was covering my now unmovable leg and stared at it, as if I was joking. I couldn't blame them. I was known to play jokes every once in a while. My mom in a barely calm voice pleaded, "Cory, just move your leg." As if her plead would magically make my leg move. I made one more attempt and told my brain to just pick my leg up. It's not complicated. My brain and leg refused to communicate with each other and my leg made no attempt at movement.

I didn't get angry or cry. I just waited for the doctor to come in and hoped he could give some type of positive news. As a naive thirteen-year-old who never had surgery before, I thought there was an off chance that I was having an odd reaction to the green apple gas. Maybe I should've picked a different flavor. I should've picked grape. I mean grape jolly ranchers taste great too.

The surgeon came into my room with a slight grin on his face, as if he knew something I didn't know. I hoped that if I pleaded with him, he could give me some magic cure that will allow my left leg to move. He has to be able to do something. He's a doctor. Surprisingly, a scary thought entered my mind. I always hated needles as a kid, but if the doctor could stick me with a magical needle that would allow me to move my leg again, I would ask for that. That's how desperate I was.

We both looked at each other and stared toward the center of our eyes for a few seconds and said nothing.

My surgeon, Dr. Charles Duncan, was a lot like me in the fact he wasn't much of a talker. He would give me short responses to my questions and short descriptions on the next steps with my health. He was my kind of guy. My mom wasn't a fan of our bromance. She immediately interjected and said, "Cory can't move his left leg." Of course, he didn't say anything and just put his eyes on my leg. He stared at my leg and asked, "Can you attempt to move it for me?" I looked at his face and assumed he was joking. Sure, he did just perform this surgery, and if anyone could magically make my legs move through communication it would be him. So, I tried. I told my brain to tell my leg to lift up. But, once again it refused to move. It turns out my surgeon wasn't the magician he thought he was.

Stepping away from my legs, he adjusted his glasses and said, "Yeah so this was a possibility with the surgery. With the position of the tumor on your spinal cord, there was a possibility that this could happen once you woke up."

Maybe I wasn't paying enough attention when my surgeon was discussing life after surgery. He could've said, "You may never walk again after this surgery." I feel like if I did hear my surgeon tell me that, I would've stayed home this morning and avoided the surgery completely. I wanted to say that I'm supposed to play recreational basketball in a week. Instead, I'm sitting here waiting for my leg to magically move. I still couldn't believe this had happened to me. In this moment I believed this surgery made my life worse instead of better. That's not how surgeries are supposed to work.

My mom and dad didn't have a response; they just stared at each other and occasionally looked at me, too. We didn't have to say anything, as all three of us knew this wasn't good.

My nurse came in with a chair that looked foreign to me as it had two metal wheels on it. Looking at that chair I thought it was for the other kid down the hall. That wheelchair couldn't have been for me. A couple of weeks earlier I had signed up for recreational basketball in my town.

Now I wasn't going to be the next Michael Jordan or Kobe Bryant with my basketball skills, so the NBA will be happy to know they didn't lose any revenue because of my surgery. But I still wanted to be on the court playing. Yes, I enjoyed the solitude of playing basketball by myself the day before my life got flipped turned upside down (The Fresh Prince of Bel Air), yet I still enjoyed being a part of a team and playing organized basketball with my friends. Now that's all gone in one day.

With one of my legs immobile, I had to grab my left leg with both arms and then swing it to left, as if I was completing a chest pass in basketball game. I guess the game of basketball didn't disappear from me completely. Kind of. I swung my foot with a surprising amount of anger. My parents looked at me in shock. What made all of this so surprising was the fact as a person who rarely showed emotion, I went from sadness this morning to anger within a ten-hour period. To be fair, I was thirteen, so I had the excuse of saying I was going through my tough teenage years. Most teenagers my age were having outbursts because of schoolwork, friendships, or relationships. My outburst was about my ability to walk.

Gripping both of the wheels, my knuckles went white with desire. (Black Sunshine by White Zombie) I started to think, would this be me for the rest of my life? I sat straight up in the wheelchair, as if I was sitting up at my desk for the first day of school and attempted to push the wheels forward. The nurse looked down at me and politely said, "No I'll bring you around today." It was finally official. I had to now rely on others. It was something I always hated ever since I could utter words out of my mouth. I always felt like asking for help was a sign of weakness, or I was being too much of a bother if I ever asked for help.

The wheelchair started to push forward, and I grabbed the handles on each side of the chair. It was a strange new feeling. I didn't want to tell her to slow down, because that gets into interacting with people. There was a small pro, as I must say I did like the freeing feeling of being away from the beeps and the entrapment of being in a hospital room.

Unfortunately, that freeing feeling of not having a care in the world disappeared quickly as I would also get glaring looks from every new face I saw. Hatred for who I had become was just beginning. I knew those looks weren't meant to make me feel bad or hurt my feelings. Looking at every new face as the wheels on my wheelchair turned, I thought about opening up to every single person. I wanted to say to each face that I was able to walk just like you this morning. I'm not really like this. I remember enjoying the act of putting one foot in front of the other. It was something so simple, the act of walking. My assumption was that I would always be walking for the rest of my life. Instead, I buried my head in shame and hated what this surgery did to me. Now I was different.

The embarrassment of seeing every face disappeared as my nurse brought me back to my hospital bed, and I was back into my room with zero eyes looking at the sick kid. I hadn't even lived a full day with my disability, and I already hated what it was like.

I went to bed in the hospital with my mom sleeping on a recliner every night. She did this every night I was away from my comfortable bed at home. A bed I already missed, even though I had only been away from it for not even a full day.

Waking up the next morning, I hoped my left leg would magically work again. It did not. I spent the entire morning staring at my leg thinking maybe things will change by the afternoon.

We did the same exact replay of yesterday with the doctor coming in and telling me we don't know if or when you'll be able to walk again. And the nurse coming into my room and rolling me around. This time was different, as I became more observant and looked around at all the faces on my floor. I didn't put my head down in shame or hate the person I had just become. I choose to embrace the curveball and embrace this new life as best as I could for at least the time I was stuck in the hospital. I kept my head up, and this time when we hit a corner and a random passerby would have to dodge my wheelchair, I would look at them and laugh as me, my nurse, and the random passerby would all apologize together for the inconvenience. Putting on a happy face really did make my day better.

Also, on this trip we would go by other rooms and I couldn't help myself, as I had to look in if a door was open. I wanted to see if I was close to the same age as any kids on this floor. I thought maybe I could become friends with some of them. I quickly stopped noticing age and started to see boys and girls who looked just as broken as I did. None of us were meant to be here. Every single one of us deserved to be in school learning during the day and hanging out with friends and family at night. Our bodies shouldn't be lying in hospital beds for 23 hours a day and waiting for doctors to tell us when we can go back to our normal lives outside. How or why did this have to happen to us? I was back to being broken.

Going to bed that night I had a feeling that the next morning could be a good day. My mom told me my brother and my friends from middle school were planning to come and visit. I needed contact with the outside world, since I had only been in contact with my parents and doctors for the past two days.

Waking up that next morning I felt inspired. The inspiration came from my brother and my friends from middle school who were taking time out of their busy weekend to come see me. It meant so much. Because of that, I was inspired and had to do my best to attempt to walk.

I wanted to walk with my friends to the common room which was only a few steps away from my room. I wanted to be a person who walked just like them. I didn't want their sympathy as I was I being wheeled to the common room. I pushed my blanket off to the side as if I was pushing away a bad meal and stared at my leg.

I stared at my leg and thought wiggle your big toe. Wiggle your big toe. (Kill Bill: Vol 1)

I turned to my mom and exclaimed, "Look, I can move my toe, I can move my toe." This was now my life, body parts moving had now become cause for celebration. She smiled and said, "That's great, now try to move your entire leg." After all of the excitement of my toes wiggling, I forgot another part of my body has been immobile over the past two days, too. I attempted to pick my leg up but it barely rose an inch off the ground, if that. I wouldn't say the feeling of disgust entered my mind. I say that because at least I had something. Two days ago, I feared I'd never walk again. Having the feeling of movement in my toes gave me some sense of encouragement. What a life.

My brother came walking in and for the first time in our friendship I didn't know what to say or do. For our entire lives we never had to think about conversations or actions. I could walk by his room and we could just give one look and that would indicate we should play video games. The same thing would happen if the weather was nice outside, as we would grab our baseball gloves and throw the ball around. At first, we would throw line drives to each other to test each other, as we both spent the majority of our time playing in the infield. We would then move to throwing ground balls to each other as we would both run to the right or left as we would try our best to sneak groundballs by each other. Finally, we would attempt to reach the sky by throwing pop-ups. Unfortunately, I knew we wouldn't be throwing pop-ups again for a while.

He started to walk into the room with a different look on his face. It wasn't the face we both grew up with as kids. It was a timid look, and I could tell he didn't know how to approach me. I thought about making jokes, about walking and standing to lighten the mood. For the first time, I wasn't quick enough or in the mood for jokes.

He stood next to me and went to shake my hand, which was our standard greeting. We didn't believe in hugs, as we were too old for that. We felt like kids much younger than us would give hugs. We knew men give handshakes, and we were men.

He reached his arm out and attempted to shake my hand. I picked up my right hand with the IV it in and attempted to shake hands. He looked at my hand and pulled his hand back in fear. I pulled my hand back in shame as I forgot about my IV. He grabbed my shoulder and said, "It's alright, I don't want to hurt your hand." I laughed as my mom brought a chair over for my brother to sit in. We went back into our normal conversations about sports and video games. It was like we were ignoring the fact I was lying a hospital bed, and that's exactly how I wanted it. We talked for about ten minutes and watched whatever was on ESPN. It felt normal. Eventually my mom butted in and said, "It's time for C.J. to leave." I was a little jealous of two things as he stood up to leave with my dad. One being the fact he could stand and walk. Two, he gets to leave the hospital.

Watching him leave did upset me, as he got to go back to his life and I had to remain stuck inside the hospital. My mom saw me going into a depressive state and said, "Your friends from middle school are coming later." That did put a smile on my face knowing my friends were taking time out of their busy lives to come and visit.

The first day at a new school is a stressful day. You have to deal with new classrooms, new hallways, and some new friends. One of the biggest worries at a new school is lunch period. Where should one sit on the first day of school?

Now the legend goes, at least in my mind, that I found a table near the stage where the middle school plays happen and the school band performances took place. My friends from elementary school found exactly where I was sitting and sat at my table. One of my friends (and he knows who he is if he's reading this book) says he started the table by sitting there first and soon everyone followed him. If someone has a time machine, please go back in time and let me know who was right.

Either way, our table was set, and the eight of my friends would sit together all three years of middle school. What was unique about my friends at the table is that they didn't watch sports as much as I did. Although there are a select few people on earth who can say they watch sports as much as I did as a kid. They loved movies, television, and video games. They would quote movies during lunch or talk about playing Halo on Xbox. I only played video games that involve sports. I would look at them with contempt and wanted to move the conversation to the New York Mets. Or talk about sports video games like MVP Baseball or Madden. Even with our minor differences our friendship never ended throughout middle school, and for them to come visit me meant the world.

A knock at my door came and one of my friend's mothers walked into the room, which I was happy to see as I didn't want my friends to see me in a hospital bed. She looked at me with a smile and said, "The boys are here to see you." My mom got out of her chair and gave my friend's mother a hug. While I sat in my hospital bed, I could see it was the embrace of two parents who couldn't believe their eyes.

The mother said, "I have the boys waiting outside of the room; where should they go?" My mom thought about it and said, "How about the playroom." The mother nodded and walked out.

For the first time I looked forward to getting out of bed. For the past two days, I didn't want to be seen or heard by anyone. I didn't embrace or plan on embracing anyone. I knew after visiting with my brother that I no longer needed to feel shame with the people who knew and cared about me. My brother, who has always been my guide through my first thirteen years of life, had showed me there's no shame in the person I had become.

I pushed my body up and into the wheelchair with a smile. I just hoped my friends would have the same reaction.

My mom pushed me out of the room and I saw my friends in the playroom. Through the glass windows I saw all seven of my friends sitting in a circle, as if they were in a kindergarten class. I had to wonder, what were they thinking?

My mom wheeled me into the center of the room and left. All seven of the faces looked up at me with a smile. I looked up and no one really knew what to say. It felt awkward as I scanned the room because I felt like a piece of art for my friends to study. My best friend in school looked away from me. I almost thought he was embarrassed by me, as we would play basketball and jump on his trampoline as kids. That wouldn't happen again for a while or maybe never. He was actually looking away to grab a giant wrapped box sitting next to him and handed it off to me. I held the box and wondered what my friends got me? I gave the box one shake and opened it.

As I unwrapped the large box, I looked at all of my friends and thought about what this moment had become. All eight of us were sitting in a playroom built for children in a hospital. An entire row of chairs built for kids much younger than us were lined up in the corner. If I wasn't the kid in the wheelchair, I would've grabbed a chair that was built for a five-year-old as a joke and pretended to sit in it. Instead, I was the kid who already had a seat.

With all of the gift-wrapping on the floor it felt like Christmas morning, and the best part of Christmas morning is seeing what you just unwrapped. I read the box, and it was a brand-new Xbox! Looking at everyone I didn't have any words. I knew this wasn't the situation any of us would ever want. We were always meant to be hanging out playing video games. You know the things all teenagers do. There should've never been a moment where one of us had to gift a system to the other while they were in the hospital. Yet it was a great moment as it showed how much my friends cared. To have people who care for you in life is a beautiful thing.

My mom was sitting at the other end of the room and walked over to grab the giant box. She said, "Wow, that's very nice of you guys." As I handed the box over to my mom, I looked at every face and said thank you.

I studied the box and saw it came with a free copy of Halo 2. I would go over to my friends' houses and lose by a lot every time we played Halo. We would have death match battles, and I would finish in last with every battle. Every loss got me closer to throwing my controller at the television. For my entire life I've hated one thing in my life and that's losing. I don't know what it was about losing that upset me so much. Could it be the days and nights my brother and I dueled that caused me to hate losing? We would play against each other, and whenever I was defeated, I would throw my controller to the ground and leave the room. I'll be the first to admit that me stampeding out of the room after every loss was very childish. I've just always hated losing. My hope was that my friends purchasing an Xbox for me would get the stench of defeat off me. I was pretty defeated at the moment.

As time continued to move, surprisingly no kids from the other hospital rooms came into the playroom. It was just the eight of us looking at each other, as if we were at an awkward teenage dance waiting to pick a girl to dance with. My best friend out of my group of friends, Mike, spoke up and said, "We can't wait to play against you when you leave." At first, I didn't look at him. That comment for the first time caused me to think about my life socially once I left the hospital. Would people look at me differently when I wheeled in front of them? How tough will it be to adjust to my new life? So many new and unanswered questions.

We looked at each other for one final time and all seven of my friends got up and walked out of the hospital and back to their lives. I wheeled my wheelchair back to my hospital bed. More pain was felt in that moment compared to when I was hooked up to machines. I say that because they got to go to back to their houses. They got to go back to their pets. They got to go back to their beds. Everything I took for granted for thirteen years, they got to continually enjoy while I had to go back to an uncomfortable hospital bed.

For seven straight days, nurses and doctors would antagonize me by asking, "Can you lift your leg for me?" After a week of attempting to lift my leg up and down, I finally got the okay to leave the hospital. I assumed being told I could leave meant I could go home and back to my life. I was wrong.

Instead, I was told I had to go to a rehabilitation center.

I didn't know what a rehabilitation center was at this point in my life. I was still a thirteen-year-old boy who had yet to experience anything major in his life. My parents were told about rehabilitation centers in the area by the staff at Yale, and they decided to choose a facility in New York. It was beyond upsetting to go from the children's hospital to a rehabilitation center. I just wanted to go back to my old life. As crazy as it sounded, I wanted to go back to school.

A gurney came into my room, and I could smile a little knowing that my journey at Yale-New Haven Hospital had ended. Never again would I have to sleep in an uncomfortable hospital bed. Never again would I have to wake up and stare at an IV in my arm. Never again would I have to hear the beeping of machines. My life was now officially past all of it.

Being wheeled to the elevator gave me a little joy, as it meant my escape was finally complete. But with that joy came a sense of fear. What will this new facility be like? Will I be able to walk again? When can I go back to school? I guess I have a lot of things to ponder. (Zoolander)

8

As my body was still in the ambulance, I kept looking for windows. I wanted to see the outside world. Had the world I missed for the past ten days changed? Are the trees still green? There were so many questions I wanted to have answered, and my hope was that peering out the windows would show me everything I had missed.

The problem was that there were no windows inside the ambulance. Instead, I just looked at my parents and the medical equipment inside the truck. The medical equipment was nothing new, as I had already witnessed what it looked like for ten straight days. All I wanted was some sense of my past life. Unfortunately, it wasn't meant to be. If I had to guess, it would probably never come back.

After being in the ambulance for about a half-hour, it came to a sudden stop. I didn't have any idea where this new rehabilitation center was so stopping now meant nothing to me. For a second I thought about how I'll be wheeled to this new facility, and I'll have to restart my life once again.

The paramedic wheeled me out of the ambulance and onto a driveway in a neighborhood with houses lined down a street. This couldn't be where the rehabilitation center is. Looking around, at first, I was disoriented by the fact I was in a random strangers driveway. All of the sudden, I looked up and there was a basketball hoop. Wait, that's my basketball hoop. I was at my house. Looking up at that hoop, I thought back to the day I played basketball at my mom's middle school. How life was so simple back then.

Back then I would've been out in the driveway for a couple of hours just shooting. I would actually play one-on-one games against my brother in the driveway. He would end up defeating me every time we played, because he was bigger and better than me. That didn't matter though because the games were just about being together and playing basketball. Like clockwork we would laugh then shake hands at the end of every game. I didn't get upset when I lost in basketball because I knew my brother was better than me. Who knew when and if we'd ever play a game against each other again?

We arrived at my house during the day, so my brother was still at school. I was curious as to why we stopped here. My thinking was that there's nothing for me in that house. It's not like I can walk in and stay there forever. No matter how long I stayed at home I was eventually going to rehab no matter what.

As I continued to stare at the basketball hoop, my mom walked through the garage. All of a sudden a small animal walked out of the garage. There was Rocky staring at me in the driveway. How did I forget about Rocky? He looked at me with the same exact look I had when I saw him after his surgery. This time the roles were switched, as I needed him to comfort me.

He continued to stare at me, and I started to yell his name. "Rocky! Rocky!" It felt very similar to the end of the first Rocky movie. The only difference was that I didn't have music playing in the background. We both stared at each other for a second, and he looked back with confusion. I could tell that he was thinking, this isn't the Cory I know. This isn't the kid who came home after school and would pet my back while I would attempt to jump and lick his face. This wasn't the Cory who would let me outside and play fetch for a half hour, and then we would sit on the couch together. I know he thought, I can't tell who this person is.

I yelled his name one more time, and he continued to stare at me as if we had never met. I put my head down, and as soon as my head went down, as I assumed, he forgot about me. When my head went down he realized who I was and came sprinting over to greet me.

He hopped onto the gurney and I started petting as he licked my face. I tried to hold him as best as I could, but he had the energy of a thousand puppies as he continued to jump all over the gurney. Unfortunately, the adventure had to eventually end at some point. It was funny as he actually sat on top of me hoping I wouldn't leave, or that he could come with me to my next journey for a couple of minutes. My mom had to pick him up and he went back into the house. That was the second toughest goodbye I had with him.

If it was possible to protest and just say that I don't want to go, I would have. I just wanted to be a teenager who goes to school, hangs out with friends and family, and spends time with his dog. Those days were in my past and now it was about starting a new future at this new rehabilitation center in New York.

As I was being wheeled into the rehabilitation center, I started to notice kids playing throughout the center. Again just as I did at Yale, I saw these kids and thought none of us should be here. All of us should be in school right now. We shouldn't be kids stuck in a rehabilitation center. Even though I was someone who stayed away from conversations, I wanted to hear every child's story. It was no longer a question about shyness; it had become a question of curiosity. Do you also have a spinal cord tumor? Did you also stay at a hospital for an extended amount of time? There was so much to know about these kids.

I was brought to a room with six beds in it and one television in the center. My bed was all the way in the right corner. Looking to my left, one bed was empty and the next bed had a child lying in it, with what I assumed was his parent standing to the left. Seeing that, I knew I would be that same child for however long I'm here. Time will tell.

The ambulance driver put the gurney next to my new bed. I stared at my new bed, which wasn't new at all, as it was the same design as the hospital bed I had at Yale. Again, I wouldn't be able to put my sleep number into this bed either. Are we at a point in writing where corporate sponsors are written into the book? I'll wait for my check in the mail.

The ambulance driver picked me up by the sheet and placed me in my new bed. He looked at me and said, "Are you all set?" I shrugged and thought there would never be a proper response to that question. I am stuck in this rehabilitation center while the whole world is still continually moving without me. I just burrowed into my bed and shook my head up and down acknowledging his statement.

I looked to the center of our room and there was the television. For all of my life the television was my giver of entertainment and all I had to do was turn it on. Unfortunately, my bed didn't have a remote connected to it so I sat and looked at the ceiling. A staff member eventually walked over to give me a schedule. She started to tell me how my schedule was going to involve schoolwork and therapy. I hadn't thought about schoolwork for two weeks. Can I still solve simple math problems? Can I still master science? Can I still learn anything?

The entire schedule was described to me and she asked, "Do you have any questions?" I replied, "Yes, could you change the channel on the television?" She laughed and said, "Yes, and what would you like to watch?" I requested ESPN, and she flipped the channel to ESPN. I didn't get the remote as it was put back on the television. I never thought I would ever miss the bed at Yale, but I did, because it had a remote that controlled the one television in my room. My perceived privilege of changing the television was now gone.

Waking up the next morning, I looked around at the five beds. Just like at Yale I continually thought, why were we here? What did we do to deserve this? All six of us seemed like good kids. Yet, we were all quarantined from the outside world inside this rehabilitation center for who knows how long.

A staff member came to my bed and told me that it was time for school. I moved up in my bed and thought about saying that I want to stay in bed. The television in the center of the room was still tuned to ESPN as no other kid requested to change it. Maybe I'll never learn anything new ever again, and I'll just live off of the knowledge I've gained through thirteen years of life. Luckily, I grew up and realized I needed school, and I went to school inside the rehab center.

A staff member wheeled me over to the classroom area and put me behind a desk. I thought back to my old life at school and how much I missed it. I remembered the thrill and excitement of finding a new seat on the first day of class. If you spotted friends in class, you would all migrate to the same area and sit together. Few things in school were greater than finding a nice desk and getting ready to learn with your friends. Now I had to stay in my wheelchair, and I migrated to no one.

Wheeled in front of a desk with five other children, the classes weren't really classes at all. And for good reason, as every single kid was coming into "class" at different levels and they were all taught at different schools. The teacher walked up to every student in the classroom and handed each of us separate assignments. Studying the assignment, it didn't seem as foreign as I had feared it would be. It was math, and I enjoyed math. Looking at the problems I thought back to elementary school. In my second-grade math class we would play speed math. I couldn't remember exactly whether that was the official title of the game. Either way I thought back to that game. One person would stand behind another student, and the teacher would read math problems off of flashcards. An example would be a teacher holding a flashcard that states '8x6=' and then a square box. The kid who was quickest to say 48 would advance and stand behind the next student. It was beyond silly to fear I had lost my ability to do schoolwork after two weeks, I didn't have anything to fear. I mean it's not like any of these spinal cord tumor cells will ever have any impact on my brain.

After my mini math lesson, I was brought to physical therapy for a half hour. The therapy ended and I went back to my room. My mother was still sitting next to my hospital bed, as she still didn't plan on leaving me alone during this traumatic experience. She looked at me and asked, "How was your physical therapy?"

I replied, "Good." She didn't ask about what I learned in school; she was just curious about physical therapy.

With an almost upset look she asked, "How long was it?" I stared at her and with a relaxing tone. I said it was a half-hour. I can see she wasn't happy with my response. I didn't think it meant anything, as I couldn't control how long therapy was.

A week would go by and half-hour physical therapy appointments would continue to happen. I didn't seem to mind, but my mom had a different idea. "Your father and I are planning on transferring you out of this facility." I didn't know transferring was an option, and I was just starting to get used to this place. That would mean I'd have to meet new people and talk about what happened all over again at a new facility. Transferring sounds terrible. I would've preferred a transfer home.

By the end of the week, a gurney came and took me out of the facility. My mom would tell me this is a great place for children who need to be here long term. You only need to strengthen your legs for a few weeks and you can get back to your normal life. We brought you here with the focus being on physical therapy; everything else we will worry about later. Because of our focus on therapy, we need to get you to a different facility. Those words were comforting as I thought the reason for the transfer was my fault.

They took me away in the ambulance, just like the week before. Picking my body up and transferring me to the gurney held the same feeling as it did the previous week. Although as I was being transferred, this time it came with a general understanding of what physical therapy was. So I wasn't as nervous as I was before.

Being escorted in an ambulance for the second time had its thrills. It was comforting lying down while a car drove me away. Obviously, my escort service was different compared to a person being driven in a limo. The oxygen masks, bandages, and gauzes weren't as thrilling compared to the bottles of champagne you would see in a limo. But it was nice to just not worry as much.

The ambulance came to a stop in front of Gaylord Rehabilitation Center. I was brought down from my stretcher, and I looked directly at the building. It wasn't a thrilling building looking at it from the outside. It just seemed like another building, and yet it was so much more, as this one had the chance of bringing me back into the real world.

Gaylord wasn't designed for me; if I had to guess, the average age of the men and women was around 60 years old. I was almost positive that I was the first teenager to ever walk/wheel into the facility. My stretcher continued to move past 60-year-olds in wheelchairs as a few of them looked at me like an oddity. And I was an oddity. I was a thirteen-year-old about to spend an unknown amount of time in a rehabilitation clinic with these people I couldn't relate to. Which was fine, because I didn't plan on relating to any of them.

The stretcher reached my room. It was everything I ever wanted, because it was a private room. There weren't five other bodies in the room and I had always loved my privacy.

My mom stood next to me as the stretcher stopped in front of my new hospital bed and I was placed gently into a new bed once again. Looking up I spotted a television and immediately turned it to ESPN and forgot about everything else around me. Before I started to focus on ESPN I asked my mom, "Why am I here?" She turned the volume down. "Look, your father's boss knows some people who run things here and he got you in." Being a naïve thirteen-year-old, I shrugged off the meaning behind that gesture. I know I'm supposed to wait till the end of the book to write acknowledgements. Well, I don't like to follow the crowd and do what every other writer does. I hope you've noticed that by now. Ben Cozzi was my dad's boss, and he got me into Gaylord. He was also the reason I got to see my dog, as he knew someone who worked with AMR ambulance. Thank you Ben.

A staff member from Gaylord came over to talk to me about the place. She started to tell us about how I'll have a full hour of therapy every weekday. There will be one half-hour of physical therapy, and another half-hour of occupational therapy. I looked up and thought, what's occupational therapy? I've always been continually told about physical therapy throughout this life-changing process. I didn't bother to ask and waited for the thrill of occupational therapy tomorrow morning. I thanked her and stayed in bed for the rest of the day. I felt like if I rested enough, tomorrow will be much an easier day.

Waking up in the morning, sadness once again came over me. I thought about how at school, I used to look out the doors before the bell would ring. Sometimes a teacher would be in the middle of his or her lesson, and they would ask that we remained seated as the bell continually rang. As a good rule follower, I would always remain seated and look through the window of the door to see students walking by. I would usually recognize one or two faces and clutch my binder knowing a recognizable face was outside the classroom. Now, people who were in their sixties were passing by the door. I just wanted to see my friends.

My mom, who still hadn't left my side, went to the door and grabbed a piece of paper that was put there either last night or before I woke up. My mom handed me the sheet and I read it as it stated I had occupational therapy at 9:30 and physical therapy at 10:30. Staring at the sheet, again I thought, what is occupational therapy?

After I sat up and ate breakfast in bed, my mom pulled my wheelchair next to my bed. It's funny, the normal way I always got up on a weekday was jumping out of bed, taking a shower, and running to the bus. Now, I was reaching for a wheelchair and lifting my body into it. Even though it was a cold day in December, I missed running to the bus and waiting in the cold for the school bus to stop and take me to school that day. There was some kind of satisfaction in waiting at the bus stop and seeing that giant yellow rectangle come down the road and stop in front of me. It always made me smile. I smiled because I was going to be brought to school to see my friends, and I was going to school to learn. Now I was going to wheel myself to therapy, instead of waiting for the wheels on the bus to go round and round.

My mom wanted to push me to my first therapy appointment, but I was no longer connected to any machines, and I was acting upset at the fact that I wasn't at school, so I dismissed my mom and I told her I'll do it. She took my marching orders well and stood behind me. I used my built-up strength that was mostly anger to push myself out of the room. I looked both ways as I crossed the hall to get to the elevator on the other side of the hallway. Although the elevator was only a few feet away, it felt like miles. With every turn of the wheel with my hands pushing me forward, I was going to face a new life once again in what felt like a retirement home.

I pressed the down button on the second floor and turned my wheelchair around and watched my mom walk to the elevator with a half-smile, acknowledging my newfound independence. It was a half-smile because she took a leave of absence from work to help me through all of this. She hadn't left the hospital or rehab over what was now fourteen days. I was always under my parent's supervision during my hospital/rehab stays. Seeing that half -smile, I knew I had to be better at acknowledging what my mom was doing. I still wheeled my wheelchair for the rest of my time at Gaylord, but I made sure I would never speed up to a point where I was out of distance from my mom.

The elevator door opened on the second floor and I rolled my way into the elevator. I made sure to press the open button to make sure my mom came with me. As I kept the doors open, a person who I had assumed was in their eighties came on the elevator with us. I didn't look at him. As we started moving, I stared directly at the number 1, acknowledging that we were heading to the first floor. I refused to acknowledge anything else. Maybe my mom and the older gentleman in the elevator were waiting for me to say something, I wasn't ready and I didn't know if I ever would be.

I rolled into the occupational therapy room on the first floor and there was already a therapist there ready to acknowledge me. I didn't have to give a name or anything. I had a feeling I wouldn't need to give my name in the future anyway, considering I was the only person who looked like a thirteen-year-old at Gaylord. And that was nice, considering I didn't ever want to say the name of the new me.

The occupational therapist stared at me for a second and said, "Hi Cory, I don't know how much we can do with you? You obviously have your parents with you when you go back home, so to re-train your body to do things around the house isn't truly necessary for you." My mom looked up and said, "It'll be nice to teach him something new." I laughed at her silly joke, as did the therapist. Eventually, the therapist stopped laughing and said, "How about this, we work on the immediate things you'll need in life and if there's extra time, I'll let you choose anything else you want." I didn't mention it, but that did hold meaning, because I was finally able to use my own voice for the first time during this rehab experience.

This being my first occupational therapy appointment, my therapist shook my hand and said, "Okay our session is over, as I'm not ready to test you yet. Let me see your schedule. You have physical therapy in fifty minutes, you can wait outside the room or go back to your room." I went back to my room upstairs while my mom stayed downstairs. I watched ESPN for a half-hour and then left my room and went back to the elevator. As the elevator came to pick me up, no one wheeled in with me. Which was a positive, as a conversation with someone who was going to most likely be at least 50 years older than me didn't interest me.

My wheelchair passed the occupational therapist office and I smiled knowing how much fun occupational therapy was and will be because of my caring therapist, and I arrived at the physical therapy area. I looked around and spotted all of the elderly citizens getting their legs stretched and learning to walk. Looking around, I thought about how much I missed gym in school. Gym was always a fun oasis from bookwork all day. In a way, this was like gym, except for the fact that no one in physical therapy room would ever think about climbing a rock wall like Spider-Man. As I looked around, I saw my mom in the corner talking with an older gentleman.

I didn't bother going over to talk; instead, I just sat at the entrance of the hall. Again, being the only thirteen-year-old in the building, my physical therapist came up to me and said, "Cory." Unable to stand and shake his hand like a proud person, I nodded my head, and the physical therapist pushed my wheelchair to a designated mat in the corner of the room.

My therapist was kind enough to lock my wheelchair in front of the mat as I threw my arms down and lifted my body onto the corner of the mat. Getting to that corner was my way of being unseen. My therapist laughed and said, "Come forward a little." Like a snake I slithered toward the therapist, and we went over what his plans for therapy were.

Sitting at the end of the table, I tried to be playful by moving my legs up and down. I moved my right leg and then forgot about the fact I can't move my left leg. I moved back up and pretended I didn't just attempt to act like I wasn't disabled. The therapist looked at me and enthusiastically told me, "I know I'm here for one reason and one reason only with you. And that's to get you walking again." I laughed. I don't know if that was proper reaction. It happened because I hadn't walked for such a long time. I didn't remember what walking was. Was it as simple as I remembered? I was pretty sure it was as easy one step forward and then follow with the next step. It has to be that easy.

This was once again an orientation session, so I got to leave early. It was like your first day of class in school when the teacher goes over the syllabus and by the end the teacher says, "I didn't have anything planned for the rest of class so just sit and wait till the bell rings." Except in this situation there was no bell. I was getting back into my wheelchair and going back to my hospital bed.

As I made my escape away from the physical therapy area, I saw my mom still talking with the older gentleman I saw earlier. I pulled my wheelchair between the both of them. I impatiently waited for their acknowledgement. My impatience grew because I wanted to go back to my room and catch up on my stories. (Wedding Crashers) But the man in the wheelchair seemed like a nice guy, so I chose to stay while this man who I assumed was in his eighties continued to talk with my mom. This man turned to me and asked, "How are you? Your mother has told me a little about you and it's nice to meet you." Looking at him I realized he was the man in the elevator. I shrugged my shoulders and said nothing. Words failed to escape my mouth. I couldn't tell you why as I had spoken with older people my entire life. It wasn't a new concept. He could tell that I was afraid to say anything and he said, "Hi, I'm Joe. I hope we can see each other in the future." I nodded my head, as I still wasn't ready for a conversation.

My first real occupational therapy appointment was a lesson on using the bathroom on my own. Something I had learned to do when I was a toddler. To be retaught that as a thirteen-year-old was beyond degrading. I thought about saying no and asking if I could be retaught something else. Options were something I no longer had.

In the bathroom there was a shower chair underneath a nozzle and a chair sitting over the toilet. This was another historically sad moment in the life and times of Cory. I should be solving math problems instead of learning how to use a shower chair. I didn't fight it though as I knew this was going to matter at some point.

I lined my wheelchair with the plastic inside this mock shower and threw my body on the plastic. I picked up my left leg and put it inside the shower, and my right leg followed easily as it hadn't grown weaker. Looking for further instruction from my therapist, she pointed toward the shower nozzle as if to say, I believe you can do this. I lifted myself up in the chair and grabbed the mock shower nozzle and pretended to spray it over my entire body, while still wearing my clothing. As I was putting the shower nozzle over my back and over my legs, I thought about how weird this was to an innocent bystander walking by. Is that kid pretending to shower with no running water while still wearing clothing? I wished I were that bystander walking by. They don't have to live with what I've been through. They are living the life I want.

After the embarrassment of the mock shower, I lifted myself out of the shower chair and back into my wheelchair. I rolled to the toilet and plopped myself onto the seat, while still wearing all of my clothing. It again had the same exact weird feeling, as I pretended to go to the bathroom and flush the toilet. Did I mention my middle school friends were probably socializing in the hallways and planning on doing fun things over the weekend, while I'm simulating going to the bathroom? Why me? I never let my emotions show as my therapist would say, "Great job," and I left the room after each appointment with no expression on my face.

Physical therapy would have the same level of excitement, but progress was slowly being made there as my therapist would continually give strength exercises for my left leg daily and my leg was slowly improving. We finally got to a point where I was given different kind of crutches.

When I got the crutches, I wouldn't say I was defeated at this point because I was making pretty good progress. I would go to both of my therapy appointments and then go back to my room in my wheelchair every night and watch television. To me television has always been my greatest escape. Although I did adore video games and playing sports as a kid, television was probably always number one on my list of hobbies. During this night I flipped to Comedy Central. As a thirteen-year-old, I was far beyond the kid's channels and into the more adult- themed channels. Channels like MTV, VH1, and ESPN. With that, I stayed around the adult channels and saw that South Park was on Comedy Central. I want this bold statement to be on the record: South Park is the greatest television show ever written. No show past, present, or future will ever be able to combine the events that happen in the real world and combine them into the scripted world like South Park has. It is without a doubt the greatest show ever. With that being said, before this night I never really took an interest in watching South Park. You try to act like a rebel as a kid and watch things you aren't supposed to watch and somehow South Park had escaped my radar. That night I kept South Park on because of one character, and that character was Jimmy Valmer. Jimmy Valmer was using the exact same crutches that I was learning to use. This may sound silly to the average person because South Park is a cartoon. Seeing someone who looked like me on television did hold value even if that person was in cartoon form. I continued to watch Jimmy Valmer as he would come into a scene, and the boys wouldn't treat him any differently. I watched Jimmy walk into a scene with his crutches and he would start to speak. Jimmy also had an issue with his speech, and he would start to stutter. I watched the entire scene as Jimmy finished all of his dialogue and no kid thought of him any differently. No kid says, "Hey, nice crutches," and pushes him down. No kid on South Park says, "Learn how to speak," and walks away. They just treated Jimmy as if he was one of the boys. I needed to be like Jimmy.

I went to my two therapies with the spirit of Jimmy inside me. After completing the bathroom sessions, the rest of our sessions became playing board games. My therapist wanted me to act like a kid, and I couldn't say no to that idea. We played Connect Four and Uno very often. When my last appointment started my therapist asked, "Do you like basketball?" I looked up at him and without crying I said, "Yes, I used to play." He could see the look of defeat on my face once I uttered that sentence. He stared at me and said, "How about we play right now." I thought he was joking, as the facility didn't have a gym and therefore no basketball hoop was anywhere in sight. He told me to follow him. I was still in my wheelchair at this point and not walking through the facility with my crutches. I wheeled myself next to my therapist with an odd curiosity, as I had no idea where he was taking me. We went into the physical therapy room and there was a giant basketball hoop bolted to the wall. I don't know how this was the first time I noticed the basketball hoop. I positioned my wheelchair in front of the hoop and started to stretch my arms. It was the routine I missed, as I used to stretch my entire body before I used to run onto the court. Of course, with that routine I was able to stretch both of my legs.

My therapist moved the treadmill that was blocking my view of the hoop and that helped give me a clear shot. My therapist found a basketball in a storage closet and threw the ball to me. It was a chest pass that I wished I had been receiving from someone who was my age, not some forty-year-old therapist in a rehabilitation center.

I started to line up my shot and as soon as the attempt was about to release my hand, I pulled the ball back to my chest as an eighty-year-old man was attempting to walk in front of me. Although there is no way of truly knowing, I imagine if you interviewed every thirteen-year-old on earth that day, I was the only one who had a moment like that. It didn't matter though because in this moment it became me and the basketball. While waiting, I continually spun the ball between my hands. A basketball had never felt so good in my hands.

Traffic had disappeared in front of me, and I was now ready to ball. I thought about dribbling the ball through my legs. But the issue was that whole standing thing, so dribbling between my legs was out of the question. I sat in my wheelchair and shot the ball, as if I was playing a recreation basketball game. But instead of dribbling the ball up court and running a play with four of my teammates, I was shooting a ball into a hoop with senior citizens stretching their legs on tables. Playing basketball at Gaylord was different as I wasn't planning on doing a pick-and-roll in wheelchair with Joe. His only contribution as he came by in his wheelchair was saying, "You've got a nice shot." I smiled, as it was nice to have some encouragement.

I took five shots while I sat in my wheelchair. I don't remember how many shots went in that day, but it didn't matter. The point of me taking those shots was that I could go back to something active I did before I became disabled. Sure, it wasn't the same as what it once was, but I did it. And that was a small thing to smile about.

I went back to physical therapy with my crutches, and we were finally getting to a point where I could leave the facility. Every time I stood up out of the wheelchair and tried to walk, I wouldn't consider the step painful. I would say the correct word was a challenge. I was putting in the work and getting to a point where I could take a step toward normalcy.

Before I left Gaylord, one my friends from Lake George came to visit. His name was Tony and he lived in New Jersey, Tony had a sister who went to Quinnipiac and the Gaylord facility wasn't very far away. I was missing so much school, the weekends stopped having meaning. When you're a kid you go to school on weekdays and look forward to the weekends with your friends. Weekends hadn't mattered until that day.

I got in my wheelchair and went to the rec room and waited for Tony to show up. Tony and my brother who was also coming by that day came through the elevator. They smiled, and the three of us sat in the rec room and watched ESPN. It was awkward to say the least as four months earlier we were playing wiffle ball in Lake George together. But for a small moment I was back to normal.

Maybe it was because we were teenagers or I was a poor communicator; we didn't say much to each other. It was pretty much hello, watch television, and goodbye. And that's the way I wanted it. As I said goodbye to Tony, I shook his hand from my wheelchair, wondering if I could ever play wiffle ball again.

I was finally told I could leave Gaylord and go home! With it came mixed emotions. I had forgotten how to function as a normal teenager. My life used to be going to movies, playing sports, and just being a teenager. Who knew if I could ever do it again? But like anything in life eventually you have to move on.

Before I left Joe came to my room and asked if I would visit him before I left. My reaction was to nod my head. This time my nod was a nod of confusion, because I hadn't really opened up to anyone during the past three weeks. It's never been in my personality to start talking with random people let alone people who were the age of my grandparents. Joe wanting to talk to me was very strange.

I wheeled myself to Joe's room, as I wasn't walking around the rehabilitation center with my crutches at this point. Joe was sitting in his wheelchair waiting for my arrival, and he held two tiny pieces of paper in his hand. He was holding two tickets to a UConn basketball game! I couldn't remember my exact conversation with Joe about UConn basketball, as all of my days at Gaylord had come together. If I had to guess, I think he saw I had UConn gear on once, and he knew I must've been a fan. It was nice that Joe would think of me as it was my time to leave Gaylord.

My dad came to pick my mother and I up from Gaylord as the transportation in the ambulance was over for now. For a normal child this should be an instance where my dad and I have this long interaction about what it's like to leave rehab. We didn't interact. I just thought about how excited I was to get back to my old life. Being wheeled in a wheelchair and smelling the fresh air was very exciting. It finally signified change and a way to move away from the past.

Getting into my dad's car and watching the green grass roll by as we sped to my house was thrilling. I say that because I had forgotten what the outside world was like. Traveling in those two ambulances rides I didn't get the opportunity to see the outside world. It had been two-and- half-months since I was in a car and just living "normal" life.

Pulling into the driveway and walking into my house with my new crutches was my first struggle back in the "normal" world.

The entrance to my house had three stairs that led to a door that officially brought you inside. For the three years that we were living in our house, I never thought about those steps. They were just steps. You walk up all three and you're in the house. There's nothing to the steps. All of the sudden those three steps became my version of climbing Mount Everest. I put my right crutch on the first step and gathered my balance. I felt stable enough to do it again. I was stabbing my crutches into the stairs with the same force as an ice climber putting his ice pick into the mountain. It was onto the next step as my crutches moved up once again. Right crutch on the step, then left crutch on the step and then lift my body. I made it to the second step. One more step and then I'm nearly at the top of the mountain. Right crutch on the third step, then left crutch and lift. Just one more little lift and I'm there. If only I had a flag to fully declare I made it to the top of the mountain. A powersauce bar flag (The Simpsons) would've been nice. I unfortunately forgot to bring my flag with me. At this point it was too late to go back to the bottom of the mountain and find my forgotten flag. At this point my main focus was getting into my house. There was just a little lift and then it was official, I was back to the comfort of my home.

After being away from my home for so long, surprisingly everything still looked and felt the same. It was like I had never left. I made my move toward the couch and everything was back to normal. Rocky wagged his tail as I approached him. We had the same embrace we always had as I touched his fur and he acted as if I didn't abandon him. His loyalty was very touching. My brother came by from upstairs. This time it was less awkward as I didn't need to shake his hand with an IV in my arm. We did our patented handshake, and I burrowed myself into the couch and turned-on ESPN.

My mom told me she communicated with my school and I could go back whenever I was comfortable. That was as meaningful as just climbing the stairs to my house was a challenge. I could only imagine what going to school would be like. My issue was I would take a lot of naps during my time at Gaylord. The vision I had was walking to class and falling asleep by the time I found my desk at every single class. The key to all of this would be my energy levels.

I spent the next few days at home doing the typical sick kid things. Watching The Price Is Right during the day and sleeping in. My time with Gaylord hadn't permanently ended, and I went to Gaylord for outpatient services. My mom was still on a leave of absence from her job as a teacher, so she would take me to outpatient therapy at Gaylord. The scar on my back had finally healed to a point where I was cleared to do work in the pool during this time. Working in the pool was the entire key to my rehabilitation success. I was given ankle weights to walk across the pool. I was told to swim back and forth without ankle weights. I would spread my legs up, down, and to the side, pushing my legs against the resistance of the water to build strength. And remarkably it did end up working within two weeks. I was done using crutches, and I was walking on my own. Sure, I still had a tremendous limp and in no way was my walking normal, but I was doing it on my own without help. The way I always wanted my life to be, one without needing any help.

By the end of that second week, I told my parents I was ready to go back to school. They didn't have any reason to doubt me, as I was always a fan of school and learning. My perfect attendance record last year was proof I didn't miss school on purpose. All I needed to do was walk, or I guess you could say limp back to school.

9

For my first day back to school, I was told I could wake up whenever I wanted. If only every school day was like that. I woke up around 9:00 AM and found my mom awake downstairs. She looked at me and said nothing. Using the power of a mother's intuition she knew I was ready to go. My confidence was high as I didn't have my crutches anymore and I could walk on my own. Sure it'll be different as I had a severe limp, but I was finally out of the hospital and rehabilitation centers. A life that was isolating was now gone.

On the ride to Hillcrest Middle School, I went back to my staring out the window phase and started to reflect on life. Will friends think of me differently now that my health has completely changed? How will that first step past my classmates go? Will I limp by all of my classmates and trip over my own feet like some kind of circus clown? The possibilities were endless. There was a small part of me that felt like I should never go back to school, because now I will have to live in a world where I had to worry about people judging me. I guess that's what comes with being different. And I guess now I was different.

I got out of the car and walked to the school entrance with my mom. She grabbed the door for me, and I walked through the middle school doors. The old life I had wanted back since that X-Ray of my curved spine was now back somewhat. I walked in with confidence, while failing to trip over my two feet—the one thing I had worried about the most. Maybe that was a sign saying that I'll be able to survive this new life of mine. Maybe.

We walked into the principal's office, and she and her entire staff greeted me as if I was as important as the President of the United States. I didn't get why I mattered at the time, so I just smiled and said hello to everyone. It felt like nothing really changed. Sure I missed two months of school, but I was still the same person. I didn't need to be treated differently by anyone. Being treated differently was something that somewhere in the back of mind I knew I would have to live with for the rest of my life. While wallowing in my self-pity, my mom left the office and let me attempt to go back to my earlier life. She finally knew it was time to let go, and I needed to start to figure my life out once again on my own.

During my visit with the principal, my guidance counselor Mr. Rago walked into the office. Before this day I never spoke a word to my guidance counselor. I never bothered to take a step into his office to open up about my life. The thought of taking time out of the day to talk with this random guy in our school never came into my mind. Why would I need to have a conversation with him? If I have an issue I'll talk with teachers, friends, or family. The job of a guidance counselor to me seemed completely unnecessary. Sitting across from him, I finally started to understand what his job was about.

Our conversation started and he stated one of the worst possible things. "Cory, you will no longer be going to gym." I never thought about no longer having gym anymore during my rehab stays. Although not having it anymore made sense, I mean a class where kids can't run, and they have to do activities that cater to people with the balance of a toddler. Does that sound like a fun class? Before I could plead for that class back, I was told I would have study hall instead of physical education. "We want you to have more time to study as your days here will be mentally draining." My disappointment still existed, but knowing how important my studies were made my disappointment start to dissipate. Just sitting in that office and talking with Mr. Rago, my body was already getting tired during our conversation. I guess the staff at Hillcrest knew what they were talking about. The next thing I was told was that I could leave classes early. The idea being when I walk through the hallway it doesn't turn into an example of The Running with The Bulls, when I attempt to dodge other students in the hallway.

Before I went to my first class, I jokingly said to Mr. Rago, "I forgot my locker combination, can we go back to the office and look it up?" We both laughed and walked back to the main office together. At least I still had a sense of humor.

Limping toward my old locker, I looked inside every classroom as I continued to walk without tripping. As I took my time, I looked through every classroom with zero reaction. I don't think anger would've been a proper reaction, but it should've at least been some type of emotion. All of these students got to continue to live their lives and got to continue to learn, while I was lying immobile in a hospital bed. I was working in two rehab centers for two months of my life while these students were having fun, having conversations in between classes and during lunch, while I was having conversations with a man in his eighties.

My glaring eyes eventually led back to my locker. As silly as it may sound, I missed the feel of turning my locker combination three times to the right, two times to the left, and one more to the right and then pulling the lock down. I pulled the lock down as if I was pulling the past two months of my life away from my memory and then unlocking a new life.

Glancing up and down the hallway as I walked to my first class, this wasn't a moment to cry about my old life, it was a moment of happiness. Although I envied all of the students sitting in the classroom, I had to be happy that I was no longer glancing at sick adults and sick children. I was going back to class instead of rehabilitation appointment. I was now looking forward to learning about math and science as opposed to learning how to re-use a shower and toilet.

I would go to my first two classes before lunch with a sense of hope. The reason hope came is because people applauded me as I walked into my first two classes. It felt very strange, as I technically didn't do anything to deserve applause. All I did was recover from major surgery for two months. It wasn't anything heroic. If the people sitting in those chairs were in my situation, they would've done the same thing. I didn't think I did anything special.

The greatest moment of my first day was going back to lunch. The thing I missed the most during my days at Yale and Gaylord was going to lunch period. I wanted those friendships during lunch period back in my life as I forgot what having my friends was like, outside of the time they visited me in the hospital. I hated having to eat my meals in a hospital bed. In the hospital and at my rehabilitation centers, I would get my meals on a rolling table. The meals would be pushed in front of me by the hospital staff, and I would sit up at the exact moment the meal would be pushed directly in front of my face. It was humiliating, and it has ruined the idea of having breakfast in bed for the rest of my life.

Because I was leaving classes early, I arrived at the cafeteria first for lunch. Looking around the room I thought about breaking down. I missed two months of memories in my final year of middle school because of a spinal cord tumor. Luckily, I was smart enough to gather myself, and I just walked back to my old lunch table and sat alone for what I hoped would be the final time ever. Could you imagine someone working in or just walking by the cafeteria seeing a child crying in the middle of the cafeteria? They would probably assume that child either loves or hates what's on the menu. I brought my lunch from home that day anyway, so the idea of me crying over the sloppy joes (Saturday Night Live) that were being prepared wasn't possible.

Surprisingly, I remembered exactly where our lunch table was two months after never sitting at my table. I guess a creator never forgets the project they created. I remembered where I sat, the first seat on the left and bent down to take a seat. The cafeteria table at Hillcrest was a standard folding table that fit eight students. The reason for the foldable tables was because our cafeteria doubled as an auditorium for the middle school band to perform on stage. The seat was nothing special, yet it was the greatest seat I had the pleasure of sitting on in the past two months. Maybe it was because I was comparing my lounging to sitting in hospital beds and wheelchairs, or there was a very strong satisfaction in knowing my friends were coming through those doors.

Kids started to file into the cafeteria, and I kept looking for the kids who came to visit me in the hospital. Remember this was a time before students carried cell phones, so I didn't text my friends to tell them I would be coming in. Even if I did have a phone then, I would've kept it a secret. I like the idea of being surprised and surprising people. That's almost always true outside of the surprise of being unable to walk after my surgery. That wasn't a good surprise.

Eventually all of my friends started to file in one-by-one as if it was a planned conga line. Not to complain, but if it was planned, I could've used a little more theater, maybe a little music.

As my seven friends started to fill the table, I shook hands with every single one of them as we both showed a strong sense of pride in knowing I was sitting at our table. The only awkward part came when the student who filled my seat for two months came back to the table with a look of strangeness. This moment became like a scene out of Game Of Thrones. I was taking back the throne. Is Game of Thrones anything like my example? I've never seen the show. I've been too busy working on this book.

Outside of the child who lost his seat to me everyone was happy I was back in school. I would walk into the rest of my classes that day and people would clap for me or shake my hand as if I was an Olympic athlete.

The school day came to an end with my mom picking me up. I knew I still wasn't ready to become a complete middle school student by getting back on the school bus with my friends. Limping to the back of the bus with the other eighth graders wasn't in the cards just yet.

With my mother staring at me she asked, "How was your day?" Looking back at her, expressionless, I said, "Fine." Maybe most kids would sit up in their seat and say it was awesome. I went to every class as if I was a rock star, and I was treated like a king at my lunch table. But for me it was fine.

Going back to school for the rest of the year felt very strange day in and day out, because it wasn't what school used to be the day before my surgery. I hated limping by the gym every day. I didn't even have to look into the gym as I did when I looked at students in the classroom; I already knew what I missing. The main activity that I missed was rock climbing. I always found fun in putting on my harness and attaching my carabineer to the harness. My gym teacher would stand in her same spot, while I took steps toward the wall and attempted to scale it as if it was Everest. My hands would go on the mock rubbery rocks placed on the wall. Holding those rocks, I would then lift myself to place my feet on the lower rubber rocks. This process would continue until I was at the top where I would ring the bell indicating I made it to the top of the "mountain." I would never do that again.

I was still adjusting to life as a person who was now declared 'handicapped.' Even though I now owned a handicapped sticker, because of what happened on November 19th, 2004, I still didn't know what being handicapped was like. For all of my life I would hold doors for older people in wheelchairs or people walking with canes. I never truly understood what their lives were like. Now the shoe was on the other foot as people were holding doors for me when I entered a building. Sometimes I would observe people looking at my legs as I walked by them. I knew what they were thinking as I walked by. How could a teenager walk as if he's an eighty-year-old man? A question I was too afraid to answer. I was now climbing a new mountain.

The greatest example of this occurred with our school security guard, Mr. Kay. To me, Mr. Kay was a scary man. For the past two-and-a-quarter years, I would observe Mr. Kay call out students in the lunch room for not cleaning off their tables or for not showing up to detention the day before. He was the typical no nonsense security guard you'd see in every school.

I left class early one day and I looked at Mr. Kay twenty steps away from me, and I realized I didn't have any identification. I had nothing stating that I had a reason to be out of class early. Out of fear, I did my best acting job ever and limped like I never had limped before. If a voter for the Academy Awards observed me limping by them they would've said, "That's one of the worst performances I've ever seen." Which is probably why Mr. Kay stopped me as I was about five feet away and said, "Hello Cory, I know who you are, and if you need anything don't be afraid to ask." With a smile I replied, "Thanks."

I would continually walk through the hallways with no conflicts, and everything was fine until I received a letter in the mail stating I was invited to the eighth-grade awards ceremony. My grades were finally in the B range in eighth grade, but they weren't award-worthy. I never received an award my entire time in elementary school or middle school. An award for me seemed like some kind of a joke.

During this time the greatest thrill for some of my schoolmates was fourth-period science class. Lunch was after science so I was allowed to leave class early and then get to the cafeteria first. This caused me to become the coolest kid in science class. Which I don't know if that's a distinction you want. Either way people I didn't even talk to before my surgery all of a sudden asked if they could escort me to lunch. I didn't even need an escort, as it wasn't that tough to get to lunch. I forgot who created this idea, but someone blurted out, "Do you need someone to carry your paper bag lunch for you?" I looked at our science teacher, Mr. Pitizler, and he shrugged while agreeing to allow one person to come with me every day for lunch. I made the same shrug that Mr. Pitizler made, as I didn't want anyone to carry my lunch. I wanted to do everything on my own. But who am I to argue?

Every single class period would became my own edition of The Bachelor. This was my first feeling of power over others. I must say it felt amazing to have power, although it was incredibly small in importance. It was nice to have that power after doctors, nurses, and therapists had power over me for two months.

I would try to do my best to give an opportunity to every student in my class. One lunch period I went with a friend who visited me in the hospital. He ended up bringing me McDonald's and we watched ESPN together. He usually received better grades than me in every class.

About that letter I received … I thought if anyone was going to get a letter about an award it would be him. My guidance counselor was nice enough to allow me to use his refrigerator to keep my sandwich and Gatorade cold until lunch. As I went to grab my sandwich I casually said, "Did you get a letter about an awards ceremony from school?" He looked back at me in shock. His look made it clear he didn't receive a letter. I didn't add to the conversation and handed my sandwich and Gatorade to him as that was a requirement to prove people weren't walking with me just so they're the first people in the lunchroom. Holding my lunch my friend asked, "Is the award you're getting for most days missed?" I don't think I told him at the time, but I really needed that joke. Ever since I woke up from my surgery on November 19th, I had been treated like a toddler. I can't say it was unwarranted as I woke up from a surgery with an inability to walk, something a toddler could relate to. I was in a rehabilitation center for two months. I'm glad my friend realized it was finally time to joke, and I laughed as we both entered the lunchroom.

The award ceremony finally came and I felt different. I had a reserved seat on the end; that way I didn't walk over anyone. It was a very kind gesture, but I didn't want special treatment. Unfortunately, I think that time in my life is gone.

The other awkward part of the awards ceremony was the fact I was in a row with straight-A students. I did start to think maybe I was getting an award for most days missed. It was the only award I could think of.

The academic awards were given without my name being called and then our assistant principal walked up to the podium while holding a certificate. She looked at me and said, "Cory Metz, we want to award you with Most Positive Work Ethic Award. We know what you've been through, and we just wanted to show you some appreciation. You've done an incredible job coming back to school." I stood up and shuffled to the assistant principal and took my certificate with a smile. She returned the smile and I shuffled back to my chair. Looking at my certificate I wondered what the word 'ethic' meant. My vocabulary wasn't that … I can't think of the word to put here. I guess my vocabulary still isn't very … It was nice to receive an award.

Before my eighth-grade graduation, I was accepted to attend Fairfield College Preparatory School. Fairfield Prep was a private all-boys high school a couple of towns away from Trumbull. I didn't really have a level of excitement when it came to attending Fairfield Prep. I applied to Fairfield Prep out of desperation. My mom thought a different school would be a nice change for me as it worked well for my brother and his academic ability. The schools I applied to were Fairfield Prep, St. Joseph, and Notre Dame of Fairfield.

I picked Fairfield Prep for one reason and one reason only. It was because I picked 'early decision' to Prep. It wasn't based off the fact I put Fairfield Prep above other schools, which the website states as the idea behind applying for early decision. If St. Joseph had early decision, I would've gone to St. Joseph. Early decision was my choice because I wasn't confident in my ability to get into any of the other schools. I thought my grades were good but not great enough to get into private schools. I ended up getting into all three schools. Because I made a commitment to Prep by choosing early decision, I didn't back out and became a Fairfield Prep Jesuit.

Before we move onto my life at Fairfield Prep, I had one final event from my previous life in middle school. It was with my friends at Hillcrest who had an end-of-the-year party. What a year it was, and to celebrate it with my friends at the end was nice. One of the highlights is that I got to dance with a girl who I always had a secret crush on in elementary and middle school. We danced for one song, and I was on cloud nine. When the party ended it should've been a moment to at least say goodbye and wish her a good time in high school. Instead, I avoided her and left the party without saying anything. Was it because I thought less of myself because of my disability? Let's keep reading.

10

I should've left Fairfield Prep. Socially it is a jock school designed for extroverts. If you play sports and you can use that as a social crutch you were fine. You would be able to go to dances at other schools with girls and life was easy for you. With my new life of awkward walking and then having to explain my awkward walking to everyone I meet and the fact I could no longer play sports I wasn't in the mood to be an extrovert. I hated who my tumor cells created.

My awkward Fairfield Prep experience started with the first day of classes and the fact that no girls were in any of the classes. When applying to Fairfield Prep I didn't think anything of the fact that it was an all-boys school. I knew there were dances with the sister school, and I was sure I would make friends who went to parties. And the fact that girls weren't in the same high school meant nothing. You never truly understand something until you're actually living it.

One of my friends who visited me in the hospital also enrolled at Prep. We would hang out for lunch with a couple of other kids, but it was nothing like my time at Hillcrest. Unfortunately, in my eyes, I never built any real friendships at Prep and I should have left.

Name the classic high school drama that defined your generation, shows like Saved By The Bell, Beverly Hills 90210, and Beavis and Butthead. One of those isn't correct. In truth, I just wanted to get the word 'butthead' in this book once with somewhat logical context. Beavis and Butthead were high school students on television, so it counts in my mind. I wasn't having the fun they had.

From freshman orientation to the last day of freshman year at Prep, every day was exactly the same. Wake up for class, my dad or mom would drive me to school. I would barely interact with any students, then I'd go home. If there were any positives to take away from this experience, every morning I went to school with my dad he would play Howard Stern. Before I get any letters or you close this book because I was a Howard Stern listener in high school, I want to make this clear: my dad would allow me to listen Howard Stern when Howard was speaking in a clean manner. To the people who aren't fans of Howard Stern and believe his radio show was all just vile potty humor and inappropriateness, you're wrong. That's not to say a teenager should be listening to him. My dad would change the station when it got to inappropriate levels.

The first major appeal was Howard Stern's ability to make my dad laugh. I would watch comedy shows on television with my dad and every time I laughed, I would look to see if he was laughing too. It was my way of judging if the show was truly funny. He would rarely if ever laugh at comedy shows. When he did laugh it was an incredibly loud laugh that would be heard through walls. That laugh let me know that what I was watching was actually funny. If I had to put an average on it, I would say at least once a week my dad would have that laugh while listening to Howard Stern. Hearing that laugh caused me to become a Howard Stern fan.

The greatest appeal of Howard Stern is his ability to interview and talk about the news. For me only one word comes to mind when I think about the show and that word is real. Whenever Howard interviews someone or talk about the news, he doesn't attempt to sugarcoat anything. He asks the real tough questions to a celebrity, and that would make you wonder: did he really just ask that? As a listener I would sit in wonderment and think, is he thinking about his future? If you ask that question, then they'll never come back on the show. And could you imagine if those celebrities went back to their agents and said, "Never put me back on the Howard Stern Show, and tell your other clients about what happened today. I'm sure they'll be just as upset as I was." That never happened as the celebrity would always answer or playfully talk around an answer. You would never read about complaints post-interview. And when Robin Quivers reads the news, no matter the story, Howard always has a smart and real response. He doesn't have any agenda. My interactions with the Howard Stern Show in the morning were the positive takeaways I had for the rest of the day.

I was never bullied at Fairfield Prep. Bullying wasn't really a thing at Fairfield Prep. Or at least I never noticed it. The faculty was good at giving out JUG to any student who acted out of line. JUG was detention at Fairfield Prep, and it stood for "Justice Under God." The champion of giving out JUG was the Dean, Mr. Brennan. If you went to Fairfield Prep when Mr. Brennan was the Dean, you can probably remember him yelling the phrase, "That's JUG. 2:30 in my office." If you were good at impersonations, you had a Mr. Brennan impression. He was a little more intimidating than Dean Pelton from the television show Community.

Looking back on it now, I'll be the first to admit that my lack of interaction with students at Fairfield Prep was my own fault, and it isn't a real criticism of the school as an academic institution. I'm not here to hate on Fairfield Prep. Actually, the real fault is the tumor cells that changed my life. There were days I could tell people were looking at the way I walked, or they flat out asked, "Are you ok?" I would graciously nod my head and say, "I'm fine." They would look back at me wanting more information. They would want an explanation from me. I would never give an explanation and either talk about another subject or look at something else implying I didn't want to talk about it. That led to zero invitations to parties or any social interactions with people inside the Fairfield Prep community.

As far as classes, I was doing around average. My grades were mostly B's and C's every semester. It was nothing to be excited about, but I didn't mind the teachers. I kept it in mind that going to high school was all about admission into college, and this was a college prep school. If they're going to help me to get into college, why leave? Plus, I didn't want to awkwardly non-explain my health situation to new students at a different school.

Every year my mom would come into my room and ask, "Do you want to stay enrolled at Fairfield Prep?" My brother was a star football, basketball, and baseball player at a different school, where he was having the typical high school experience. He was coming home from parties at midnight and hanging out with friends on the weekend. While I was just sitting in my room playing video games, doing homework, or listening to replays of The Howard Stern Show on satellite radio. It was the definition of a reclusive life. Yet, every year my mom asked about transferring my reply would be, "No I don't want to transfer, I want to stay at Prep." I could've gone back to my public high school if I really wanted to. I could've seen my old friends; they would've known the 'old' me, so I think that could have been the perfect situation. A second thought was, would those same friends have looked down on me? I would've been seen as the kid who moved on and came crawling back. I thought of my old friends as people who wouldn't want any part of me. I couldn't go back to the old life. Besides, a new life was starting for me anyway.

11

Have you ever had painful headaches? The common way to end a bad headache is popping a pill into your mouth and then the headache is gone. I started to develop bad headaches in December of my senior year. They wouldn't exist during the day and then out of nowhere they would appear after school. I would go up to my room close the door and stay in the dark all night. Being alone in my room in total darkness was the only solution. The headache can only be described like a ringing alarm clock going through my brain. The headache would eventually disappear in the morning and I would be able to get up and repeat this process every day.

Eventually it got to a point at night where I'd limp to bed and bang on my bed as if I was King Kong because the pain was so bad. I started taking Advil to relieve the pain. The pills, along with sleeping, would allow me to barely survive most nights.

I still went to school because this excruciating pain would only come at night. One December morning I drove to school and I can still remember the exact spot this happened. It was the downhill slope after the entrance ramp of Exit 46 going South on the Merritt Parkway. It hasn't—and I don't think it will ever—escape my mind.

I was in the left lane when all of the sudden it felt like I was struck by lightning for about three seconds. In that moment I didn't have control of my body or the wheel of the car. If a passenger was sitting next to me, they would've been freaked out as it would've looked like a ghost was driving the car. It was a miracle the car stayed straight and I didn't crash into the guardrail. In a state of panic, naturally, I turned my radio down because there was no other logical thing to do in this situation and started to think about what just happened. If I don't hear Howard Stern talking to me, then maybe things will start to make sense. It was a sunny day, so I knew I couldn't have gotten struck by lightning. Unless there's some new form of lighting that appears without a cloud in the sky. My mom's middle school was only two minutes away from Fairfield Prep and not knowing what just happened, I pulled into Fairfield Woods Middle School and called my mom. She answered the phone knowing I was on my way to school.

With terror in her voice "Cory!" My mom knew I was going to school so me making a phone call this early must've indicated some kind of an emergency. I took a deep breath in and I barely managed to utter the sentence, "I think something bad just happened to me." "Something bad, what does that mean, exactly?"

"It feels like I was just struck by lightning."

"Struck by lightning, what does that mean, where are you?"

"I'm in front of your school."

"Okay wait there for a minute, and I'll tell the principal I need to leave."

I patiently sat in my car, as my mom stayed true to her word came out in a minute. As long as you define 'patiently' as nervously shaking your hands on the steering wheel as if you had seen a ghost.

My mom ended up bringing me to Yale-New Haven Hospital, figuring the pain I was suffering from had to mean something. I explained the pain to Dr. Duncan and he said, "Take more pills for headaches. We can't figure it out." I knew he tried as Yale-New Haven Hospital is one of the best hospitals in the world, and I can't blame him for his attempted diagnosis. He has been with me throughout the past four years, if he didn't get it no one will. A random three-second episode and random headaches I imagine never appeared in any medical textbook. As we left my mom said, "There must be something here." I nodded and continued to live my life.

During this time, I was applying to colleges and universities. My grades at that point were good; the same was true about my SAT scores. I sent applications to 12 schools. Only two of those applications would end up mattering to this story. One of those applications was to Manhattanville University. There wasn't much to my application to Manhattanville. It was close to my house, and my SAT scores were within range. I had a scheduled interview with Manhattanville on a Saturday morning. My alarm was set Friday night, and this shouldn't be a part of my story, yet somehow it is.

Saturday morning came without me waking up. The next few paragraphs have been re-told to me.

The alarm kept ringing and ringing, while my eyes never opened. My mom heard the alarm and knew I was leaving to go on an interview that morning. She opened my door and saw I wasn't waking up. Like every kid, I would have some mornings where I needed help waking up. My mom assumed this was one of those days. She pushed my shoulder, alerting me of the fact it was time to wake up. I still didn't move my eyelids. Now my entire body was starting to shake. Immediately my mom yelled, "Craig (my dad's name), he's not waking up, call 911!"

A stretcher was brought to my bedroom on the second floor. The paramedics came and failed to wake me up. With that I was put on a stretcher and brought to Bridgeport Hospital, a division of Yale-New Haven Hospital. The staff at Bridgeport Hospital took a look at me and put me in a corner while making a phone call to Yale. I wasn't a patient of Bridgeport Hospital, so what to do with me was a mystery to them. And like an episode of ER, Grey's Anatomy, or Scrubs, the Bridgeport staff came and rolled me out of the hospital and I went to Yale.

Even at Yale, what was wrong with me was a mystery to them. My body was shaking up and down, I was yelling to myself and attempting to rip my clothes off. Think of this like a musical festival minus the music.

 I was brought to get a CAT scan as some type of imagery of my brain may solve the issue. Before the CAT scan, a doctor lifted my eyelids and noticed there was an issue by just staring into my eyes. They brought me back to my room and punctured my skull with a brain shunt. Once the brain shunt was placed, I was put on a life-support machine.

After two nights in the ICU, I woke up and started to keep my eyes open. As my eyes finally stayed open, I noticed the two people sitting in front of me. They started to talk with me with smiles, as I was finally keeping my eyes opening. A doctor was brought in and asked, "Do you know where you are?"

"No."

"You're in Yale-New Haven Hospital."

"Do you know the two people standing to the right of me?"

"No"

"They are your parents."

I smiled knowing my parents were there. Ten seconds would pass.

The doctor asked, "Do you know where you are?"

"No."

"You're in Yale-New Haven Hospital."

"Do you know the two people standing to the right of me?"

"No."

They are your parents. This process was repeated a few times. The difference was what seemed like every nurse on staff would come by and ask those two questions. With every new face, I would become more and more frustrated as it started to feel like I lost my mind. In a way I did.

12

I was wheeled out of the ICU and brought back to the children's
section of the hospital. Looking out my door and seeing a front desk
with a receptionist taking calls, it all started to make sense. The
feeling of being here before came over me. Things hadn't changed
much four years later. I just had one question: why am I here?

Dr Duncan was in shock as he wondered why I was in the hospital.
If my brain could process something to say to him, I would say
something. It's just the whole processing things wasn't really in my
game plan at the moment.

He looked at me and said, "It looks like there was something wrong
with you." We will run some tests and hopefully we will be able to
release you soon.

For the next three weeks of my life, I was lying in bed and kept
getting memory tested every day. The exact opposite of what you
want to do your senior year of high school.

Here's an example of a memory test. Now imagine getting this test from multiple nurses and doctors daily:

"I want you to remember the word 'orange'. Now I'm going to tell you a story, and by the end of the story tell me that word.

I walked into the mall not knowing what I wanted to purchase. I walked into a few clothing stores: Gap, Old Navy, and Abercrombie. I started to try on a few outfits from each store, but nothing satisfied me. Unsatisfied with my shopping experience I tried to find pleasure in the food court. Going to the food court I found a slice of pizza at Sbarro. I thought, I'm going to get me a New York slice. (The Office) There was some satisfaction in that, but I wanted more. I went to the video game store GameStop and bought myself a brand-new videogame. I was now satisfied. I went to the mall and I conquered my goal in purchasing an item. I left the mall fulfilled. What was the word I mentioned at the start of my story? Without cheating, did you remember orange? Don't lie. This test was given to me at least once a day. After about three days of tests, I wished my next tests were in chemistry or some other subject I was studying in school, instead of another memory test.

Another annoying test I would be given daily was the 'flash of light in my eyes at a random time' test. I don't think that was the proper name, but hey, why not? I couldn't be upset by this test as it had the possibility of saving my life. The worst part was the random hours that the test would be administered. I would be sleeping and a nurse would walk in and nudge my shoulder.

"Hi Cory, do you mind if I check your eyes?" I made sure to always nod yes and smile. Although waking up at random hours wasn't ideal and I wanted to yell, "No don't bother me." I knew the nurses were just doing their jobs, and I had to respect that.

There were times that I would be woken up at 12:37 AM. Being awake at that time it would be tough to go back to sleep, so I would scroll through my television and for the rest of my hospital stay if I were awake at that time, I would watch Late Night with Conan O'Brien.

In 2008-2009, late night television was a little simpler. My brother told me the best guy on late night was Conan O'Brien. Being up at 12:37AM, I remembered this and put on NBC, while my mom slept in an uncomfortable chair next to my bed.

To me what made Conan O'Brien the best is the fact he rolled with the punches. When he makes a bad joke, he pauses and attempts to save the joke by explaining how it can be seen as funny. If that fails, he laughs it off and moves to his next joke. Conan has an attitude that says to keep going until you've truly known you've failed. I hope Conan O'Brien can appreciate my commentary.

Three weeks in the hospital would go by as fast you could imagine three weeks in a hospital would go. It wasn't all bad as my guidance counselor from Fairfield Prep came to visit and gave me reassurance with my standing in life. "Well, all of your applications for colleges are in and once you're back to school, I believe you'll be ready for college." I got lucky because this health complication happened after the college application process finished. So, I was to go through 'Senioritis' inside a hospital. Senioritis is fake disease I wish I was fully engaged in at school. Instead, I was experiencing it from a hospital bed while suffering from a real disease.

The friends who I didn't think I had at Fairfield Prep ended up visiting me at the hospital. Andrew Lucille and Andrew Vanam. Throughout my three-and-a-half years at Fairfield Prep, I thought they barely knew I existed. We weren't friends. We knew of each other, but we never had extended conversations together. For them to take time out of their nights was very meaningful. We talked about school, and then they left to go back to their lives.

Another person who I assumed was just a casual acquaintance of mine was Anthony Mingello. He brought a New York Mets program from the 2009 season. Anthony and I would discuss the Mets throughout our high school career. The Mets ended up missing the playoffs in 2007 and 2008 in ways that only made sense for the Mets to pull off. I can go through a description of what happened those two years, but like a good Mets fan, I don't talk about the past. I thanked Anthony and looked through the program with the hope 2009 would be better. I mean, 2009 had to get better for me and the Mets, right? We didn't talk about my illness or school. We just talked about the Mets and a belief that this may be a great year.

My three weeks came to an end and I went back home. Dr. Duncan told me there were tumor cells on my brain and that'll need to be monitored. This time leaving the hospital had a different feel. This time I wasn't going to a rehabilitation center after my hospital stay. Which I guess was a positive in all of this. But, I was going to school where I felt like an outcast. Although three "friends" from Fairfield Prep came to visit me, I still didn't believe people cared or even knew me at Fairfield Prep, compared to middle school where I knew I had friends.

After my release from the hospital, my parents weren't comfortable with me driving to school, yet. My dad brought me to school and played Howard Stern on the way there. That made me smile and did give me a little less fear when it came to once again going back to school as the 'sick kid.' I came in a little after the morning bell and entered through the cafeteria doors. There weren't any balloons or a marching band for me as I walked in. Probably because Fairfield Prep didn't have a band. I guess I was right; they don't care about me after all.

I walked up to the dean's office to tell Mr. Brennan I was back. He was the man who scared me, as I truly didn't know the man and I didn't think he knew me either.

There he was sitting at his desk looking through papers. Something I didn't know he did, as I never visited his office. Once I was spotted, he forgot about his papers and stood up to greet me. "Cory, it's good to have you back." I was smiling as hearing the word 'back' always held a strong feeling in my mind. I was back out of the world of the children's hospital. The world I had suffered through for the second time in four years.

The conversation ended with Mr. Brennan telling me that Mr. Magdon would like to meet me. Mr. Magdon was the headmaster at Fairfield Prep. He was also the head football coach at Fairfield Prep. For obvious reasons, I had no reason to know Mr. Magdon. Believe it or not I wasn't the starting quarterback at Fairfield Prep, and as the residential kid who does nothing in high school, I didn't go to football games as a fan either. He was a just some dude to me. (Seinfeld) I was fairly certain he was that guy with a mustache.

Mr. Brennan placed a call to this mystery man. "Hello, Richard. Cory Metz is here." I still wasn't 100% confident in the person who was walking into the room. I wouldn't call myself Sherlock Holmes when it came to solving mysteries. And if you did call me Sherlock Holmes it would be Will Ferrell's version of Sherlock Holmes.

Five seconds after Mr. Brennan's call was placed, a man came walking into the office. I assumed the man was Mr. Magdon. I went to give him a handshake as most men do. He disagreed with that and gave me a hug instead. For about five seconds he hugged me and said, "It's great to have you back. We were worried about you. Before you get settled and go to your classes, I want you to sit in my office." I followed Mr. Magdon, still confused by who he was exactly and amazed by the fact his office was only five steps away from Mr. Brennan's office, something I hadn't discovered the past three-and-a-half years as a student at Fairfield Prep. A little embarrassed, I took a seat in Mr. Magdon's office.

Mr. Magdon's office was unique as it was loaded with televisions that had security camera feeds. As the headmaster, he was in charge of security and making sure everything was up to snuff at Fairfield Prep. Now, I finally understood what he did at Fairfield Prep. He looked at me and spotted my tie. It was a New York Mets tie. At Fairfield Prep we had to wear school uniforms: a collared shirt, dress pants, dress shoes, and a tie every day. The only thing that allowed you to express your personality in wearing my school uniform was my ability to have a wacky tie. I wish we had a Hawaiian shirt day on Friday. (Office Space) Mr. Magdon said, "Is that a New York Mets tie?" I smiled, "Yes, it is." "Alright, I want you to come to my office whenever you feel like and talk about the New York Mets. I prefer you come every day, but if you can't do that it's fine."

Every day I was too shy and I didn't want to be much of a bother to Mr. Magdon and go to his office. Every day Mr. Magdon would usually come up to me and in the nicest way possible raise his voice and say, "Metz, where have you been? Come to my office tomorrow morning." This would happen more than I would like to admit. I always made sure to show up that next morning.

Coming back to Fairfield Prep was the same as Hillcrest Middle School. I would get applause from students and teachers that I deemed unwarranted, but still happily accepted. Teachers would ask me how I was feeling. I would give simple answers like fine. A patented Cory Metz response to any question about my health.

The second day I came back to school was the day of Barack Obama's inauguration. My history teacher deemed this to be an important moment related to history, so she allowed us to abandon the lesson of the day and watch the inauguration. Watching his inauguration didn't really impact me that much. I was 17 at the time. I didn't go to the polls and cast my vote for the president. Teenagers aren't into politics, and it's not like I will ever meet the man.

A few days later I got an important phone call that I didn't know at the time would change my life.

I was in my dad's car and all of the sudden a phone call with a random number appeared on screen. He answered cautiously as he usually has direct contact with everyone he speaks with.

"Hello."

The voice on the other end of the line said, "Hi, Mrs. Metz. This is Melissa Laguzza from Fairfield Prep."

"Hi, this is her husband, you called the wrong number."

"My apologies, I picked the wrong number out of the directory."

"I can give her number if you like."

"No I have it here, I just picked the wrong one. I'll try that one now."

"Okay."

"Thank you."

My dad ended the call and I looked up with a strange curiosity. I asked, "What was that about?" He looked back at me and in a patent sarcastic tone, "What the hell do I know, she called for your mother." The inspiration for all of the comedy in this book comes from my dad. Peyton and Eli Manning become two of the greatest football quarterbacks in the NFL with the help of their dad, and I become a person who writes this book. Who wins?

About two weeks after that call, my mom came into my room and pushed my feeding tube to the side of the room. You're probably wondering where that feeding tube came from. Sorry I forgot to mention that. I've also been diagnosed with Crohn's Disease. You know those commercials where the actors and actresses search for the bathroom when they're out in public. That's me everywhere I go. It's just that my life doesn't come with a voiceover telling you about the drug. It makes eating a living hell for me. Every time I sit to have a meal it takes me forever to consume the food. I would say the time it's most annoying is when I go out to eat and everyone finishes their meal in a reasonable time, while I'm still eating my meal alone. I have one story about crohn's disease that I think sums up the disease well for everyone who suffers from it. This happened in Lake George, New York, with my brother along with Tony, who was the friend who visited me at Gaylord rehabilitation center in case you forgot. Remember, I'm here to help you.

We went to the Wind Chill Factory, a local place that has pretty good chicken fingers and french fries. Before we left, my parents told my brother to make sure Cory finishes his food and eats everything. Like a good brother he took those words to heart and stared me down as I ate my chicken fingers and french fries. My eating that day kind of reminded me of one of our epic ping-pong matches. Whenever one of us would serve, we would look at each other and make sure the other one was ready. My brother was staring me down. Eating became a game for me. Eventually I got to a point where my stomach said stop. So, I stopped eating. My brother remembered the words of my parents and told me to finish the food.

I said, "I couldn't."

In a rallying cry C.J. and Tony both began to slam the table and cheered the words, "Eat it."

"Eat it."

"Eat it."

As if we were in an arena and my consumption of this last chicken finger earned me some kind of trophy. I heard the crowd's roars and ate that final chicken finger and my meal was now finished. My brother said, "Good job, I'll throw your plate out for you." Turning away and out of sight, he went to the trash, and as soon as he was gone a bad feeling came into my stomach.

Tony looked at me and asked, "You alright?"

I laughed as there was no possible way I was going to throw up. I felt perfectly fine all day and two seconds before I ate that final chicken finger. What couldn't have been two seconds later some of the chicken fingers disappeared on the table. Tony jumped from the table as if he was a grasshopper. I immediately turned away from the table and attempted to make it the woods. I had one last hurl and that was it. I looked to the side and my brother started to grab napkins as he knew I was throwing up. He shrugged and said, "What happened?" Tony was laughing as was I, and I said, "I told you I couldn't eat more." And that's why I don't enjoy the song We Will Rock You by Queen or participate in cheers where the Jumbotron encourages fans to bang their hands together.

Back to the original story, the conversation started, and I was confused by mom entering my room as she rarely did on weekdays because I was always consumed with schoolwork. She told me to stop what I was doing as we needed to talk. She told me "Your Spanish teacher and I have been in contact with the Make-A-Wish Foundation, and you'll be having a wish." I immediately touched my entire body thinking, is there something I don't know? Before I asked my mom she reassured me, "This doesn't mean anything bad for you. The foundation just wants to make you feel better after what you've been through." I had the assumption that kids who were involved with the Make-A-Wish Foundation were fighting for their lives. That's not true. The mission statement of Make-A-Wish is to grant the wishes of children with life-threatening medical conditions and to enrich the human experience with hope, strength, and joy. I was still cautious, as I had no idea what being a Make-A-Wish kid really meant.

Acceptance letters to universities and colleges started coming in my mailbox. For some reason I applied to Southern Connecticut State University. The school wasn't recommended to me by my guidance counselor. I thought that since my mom went there, she could tell me more about the school if I went there. There wasn't any sound logic in my application.

In the end it became my most important application, as the school was in New Haven, the same city as Yale. I played it safe and chose Southern. The other schools I applied to that were across New England and New York failed to matter. In my eyes, for my own safety, I had to stay close to New Haven. Southern Connecticut State University would be the university I attended in the fall.

☐

13

My dad ended up knowing the contractor who built Citi Field, which in 2009 was the new home of the New York Mets. My dad, mom, and I (my brother was in college) went to a reception for the construction union that helped construct Citi Field. A man there handed my dad four tickets. Then my dad handed me those tickets and the look and touch of paper never felt so good. The New York Mets on opening day at a brand-new ballpark. What a dream. This is going to be amazing.

I invited Anthony Mingello to the game as we had four tickets. With my brother in college and Anthony being the person who took time out of his life to visit me in the hospital to discuss the Mets, it made sense for him to enjoy the game with us. They say once baseball starts in the Northeast then you truly know seasons have changed. The cold bitterness of winter is gone once you here the two words play ball. If anybody in that stadium had the desire to be truly bitter of what the past winter meant to them it was me. Although I didn't know the stories of all of the 48,000 fans in attendance that day, I'm pretty sure my story was up there in terms of people who needed this moment. I needed something to look forward to and being outdoors watching the New York Mets was that moment. The New York Mets would end up losing 6-5 against the San Diego Padres. The results didn't matter that day. What mattered was the fact I was outside enjoying life. Something I had lost in my days in a hospital bed.

A week after my trip to see the New York Mets open Citi Field, my mom told me two people from the Make-A-Wish Foundation would come to my house. I found the idea of two people just randomly coming to my house strange. Who are these people?

A car pulled into my driveway and sat there for what felt like hours. I ran to the window and yelled, "Someone is here." As if it was Christmas morning. Even though it was the middle of April and there wasn't a speck of Christmas snow on the ground.

Sitting on my couch I spotted a second pair of lights going by and immediately jumped off my couch to stare at the two cars sitting in the driveway. What occurred after was a moment that's been stuck in my brain ever since those two people stepped out of their cars.

My doorbell rang and although this moment was really for me, I let my mom open the door. I was in her house after all. I'm also afraid to meet new people, if that's not known by now.

The door opened and two smiling faces walked in.

"Hello, I'm Cathie," one voice stated.

"Hi, I'm Georgianna," the other voice said.

They were both all smiles as they spotted me and at the same time they both said, "You must be Cory." I smiled back and shook my head up and down. My favorite lack of a reply that I could think of.

We walked together to the dining room where my mom put out a cheese plate. It was a nice touch.

We all sat together at the same time and Cathie pulled out a folder with a few papers. She asked, "Do you know anything about Make-A-Wish?" For my entire life I've been a fan of the television show SportsCenter on ESPN. As a kid, I would wake up to watch the 6 AM SportsCenter to see the previous night's result. Back in my day (The Dan Le Batard Show) smart phones weren't a thing and the quickest way to get sports results was watching SportsCenter. They started to do a segment called 'My Wish,' and I watched the segment when it started in 2005. Having my spinal cord tumor in 2004, I kind of understood what the segments were like when they showed the kids in the hospital losing out on their childhood. I never thought I would ever be one of those kids.

"I know ESPN does a Make-A-Wish series called 'My Wish.' I've seen them all." As if Cathie was going to give me a gold star for watching television. "That's great, Disney/ESPN does great work for us."

"Do you think I can be on the show?" They both smiled together and Georgianna interjected, "We'll see what we can do."

"Just to give you a little more detail on Make-A-Wish. Georgianna and I are here to get you to your one true wish. The one thing you've always wanted. We'll do our best to make that happen. Do you have any ideas?"

Nobody has ever asked me what my one true wish is. There's so much to think about in that one question.

At first, I shrugged my shoulders, as I couldn't think of a wish.

Cathie grabbed a piece of paper. "It's ok. Not every wish kid has an idea in the first two minutes. I'm going to have you fill out an 'All About Me' form. This form will allow us to understand you more and possibly help get you to a wish." I grabbed the form with doubt as I didn't think a form could answer the question of, what is my true wish?

We went through the form together. I filled out that my favorite color is green. For my favorite book/story I said Of Mice and Men. Maybe it wasn't Of Mice and Men. That question meant so little to me. I just thought about the last high school book I read. It could've possibly been The Great Gatsby. Whatever it was that question didn't matter. The most important question came next.

Who's your favorite athlete? It only took me a second to put pen to paper and write the name out, I had the name in mind. David Wright.

From the first day David Wright was called up from Triple-A, I enjoyed watching him play. David Wright was the All-Star third baseman of the New York Mets. His first full season was in 2005. From 2006-2008, he made the All-Star game each year. Although when I played baseball as a kid I played second base (because it was the easiest position when it came to throwing the ball to first), in my early Little League days, I would rotate to third base sometimes. I remember how tough those throws from third were. I would watch David Wright make Gold Glove plays, and I admired what he was doing. If there was anyone I would like to meet it was him.

Cathie looked my way and asked the million-dollar question once again, "What do you want your wish to be?

In a true Cory Metz fashion, I went in a completely different direction and said, "I want to meet Howard Stern." I wanted to be in the grace of The King of All Media. After the many hours of listening to his voice through speakers, I wanted to see him in person. A desire to shake his hand and sit in his studio. Maybe I can go on air during the news.

All four people sitting at the table stared at me with shock. I could tell they were thinking, out of all of the ideas on the planet, and that's what he thinks of! Wait, actually my dad had a smile on his face, since he loved The Howard Stern Show ever since he came to Hartford. My mom knew about my fascination for the show, but she was smart enough to say, "Keep thinking."

Cathie jumped in again. "You talked about ESPN earlier. Why not do something in sports?" Something in sports made sense. I listed out the three major sports I watch and my favorite teams in each sport. NBA, MLB, and NFL were the leagues. The New Jersey Nets, the New York Mets, and the New York Giants were my teams. I can't remember who said it, possibly, Georgianna, Cathie, or my mom. One of them mentioned asked if I wanted to do it big. Something so out of this world that I would never get a chance to repeat it and would never forget it.

With that, I crossed off the idea of meeting my favorite team. Meeting a single team was too small. If I wanted to go big, I should pick from the All-Star events. That way I can see the best of the best. I thought about the three major sports leagues that I followed. I chose Major League Baseball. With David Wright being my favorite athlete and remembering going to the first game he played with the New York Mets , that was the only wish that made sense for me.

"I want to go to the MLB All-Star game." Georgianna and Cathie were both happy because I was so confident in my answer, after my early struggles.

Cathy wrote down MLB All-Star game and thanked my parents and I for allowing both of them in our home. Georgianna smiled and repeated the same praise.

As we stood together saying goodbyes, I took one final look at the both of them thinking that what they did tonight was pretty incredible, for these two people to take time out of their busy schedules on a weekday night to visit me. I can only hope to be like them one day.

Back in school, I was told that I would be receiving an award at a ceremony for Fairfield Prep seniors. I had a feeling it would be similar to my Hillcrest Middle School award experience. Just a quick certificate and that's it. I didn't deserve more.

The award ceremony came with zero nerves. I didn't think much would happen. The ceremony was at a large church in the town of Fairfield. It wasn't in Alumni Hall at Fairfield University where we normally held mass. Maybe this was a big deal.

I walked in with my parents, and we found a row in the middle of the church. There were about thirty rows, so it was a bit of a walk for me to walk all the way to the alter to receive my award. With my walking disability still in existence this was a great risk. I did do one thing right that night; I made sure to sit at the end of the row. Ever since November 19th, 2004, I worried about walking in every new situation I faced. Whether it be going into the cafeteria or going to a sports event. I always needed to be on the end so I don't have to walk over people and risk tripping over my feet. If I couldn't find an aisle seat, I would leave. Cory Metz doesn't want to look like a fool in front of others.

The academic awards went first to the students who were a lot smarter than me. Then I started to hear our principal talk about giving away the Mark Messoli Award, an award meant for the student who shows the most courage over their four years at Fairfield Prep. Dictionary.com defines the word courage as the quality of mind or spirit that enables a person to face difficulty, danger, pain, etc., without fear. Bravery. I guess the moments I had in the hospital have allowed me to be considered for this award.

"Cory Metz." I stood not thinking it was a big deal. I just lived my life once again. I didn't want any fanfare or acknowledgment. I looked forward toward the alter worrying about tripping and not acknowledging the people around me. Left foot, right foot, left foot. (Family Guy) Why did I sit in the middle of the church? I made it halfway to the alter without tripping. I started to smile, and a sudden rush went through my body, as Mr. Hanrahan, my guidance counselor who sat at the alter and visited me in the hospital, stood up to clap for me. He was one of the nicest faculty members on staff, and I greatly appreciated his encouragement. As he stood, the remaining four faculty members in the front of the church stood and clapped. I was too worried about failing to recognize who these four people were. Focusing my view on our principal, I saw he was holding a small plaque. I always questioned if I was ever plaque worthy. And today I can say I am. (The Simpsons)

Shaking hands with our principal, Father Hanwell felt weird. This was the first time we met. All of my contact had been with Mr. Brennan and Mr. Magdon as far as administrators. We shook hands and he told me to turn around as a photographer was going to take a picture of the both of us as I held my award. I turned and stared at the audience.

Everyone in the church stood and clapped for me. Have you ever received a standing ovation? Whether it be one person or 50,000 fans in the stadium, I believe we all deserve a chance at a standing ovation. Spend your life doing great things and I believe you will get one, if you haven't. You're on your way to doing great things by reading this book.

I smiled for the picture and walked back to my seat while the applause continued until my body was back in the pew. I guess the students and staff at Fairfield Prep always cared about me. I just failed to recognize it.

Graduation at Fairfield Prep came and went. I wore an all-white outfit that every student graduating wore. Sitting and waiting for my name to be called by our principal, I reflected on the past four years.

I thought to myself, should I have gone to my local public high school? The past four years were the loneliest times of my life. How different would my life be if I just said, I want to go back to my public high school with my friends from my middle school? Life comes with a lot of 'what if' moments. My 'what if' moment was now in the past, and I had to live for the future. The past is the past. I grabbed my high school diploma and looked forward to college.

14

Before college started, I had my 'wish trip' to look forward to. My wish referral was in April of 2009, and miraculously I got to go on my wish that summer. Most kids have to wait longer as scheduling is always tough with travel wishes. Before every granted wish, Make-A-Wish kids get wish delivery parties, a party for kids to have a mini celebration before they go on their trip. A majority of the parties happen at restaurants. The restaurant I picked was Outback Steakhouse. I've grown quite fond of that place. (Step Brothers)

As we drove there, I thought to myself, what will this party be like and is it necessary? I hadn't really done anything to deserve a party. I picked a wish and it will be happening. What's there to celebrate?

I had eaten at Outback Steakhouse countless times since they opened nearby in Shelton. I would get a nice steak and a Hi-C pink lemonade. The key to life is consistency, and I would nail that order every time. I probably could've been identified as the 'steak and pink lemonade kid' when I walked in. This time was different though as I was being identified as a wish kid and not the kid who placed the same order.

Once we entered, Cathie and Georgianna were there to greet me with a smile. Their ability to be timely with everything and to have a smile both times we met was very encouraging. The only thing I really thought about was my steak. Georgianna had different ideas and told me to go outside for a picture. What is this, high school graduation? I don't take pictures. As I thought about saying no to Georgianna, I thought about what she was doing for me. The time she was putting in for me. Although I didn't know what her story was in terms of helping the foundation, I knew she was taking time out of her day to help me. Because of that sacrifice, I would do anything she needed that day. I walked to the entrance of Outback and smiled to take a photo with my parents.

We walked to our table, and I spotted some bags being carried by Cathie and Georgianna. The bags weren't important as I was worried about placing my order as our waitress approached. Although I always ordered the same thing, I still wanted to focus and nail my order.

The waitress followed us as we walked to our table, as I'm sure Cathie or Georgianna called Outback and told them about me, and management was making sure that I was taken care of. That was very impactful. The waitress looked my way and I hesitated, as I usually get nervous when I place my orders at restaurants. I can't put my finger on why it's an issue exactly. Thinking about it being in a small group, while others await your decision puts pressure on me. There must've been some silly childhood mistake I made with placing an order that has caused this feeling. I guess it comes down to speaking in front of others. I hate doing that.

With orders being out of the way, Cathie and Georgianna put presents on the table. I thought about saying that the presents were completely unnecessary. I'm already going to the game; you don't need to increase the experience with gifts. But where are my manners? Presents are presents, and when they're offered to you, you open them. It's common curiosity to accept them.

The first gift was the book called 101 Reasons to Love The New York Mets. If you're a true New York Mets fan, you're most likely laughing at that title right now as most fans have a love/hate relationship with the New York Mets. From the inception of the New York Mets franchise in 1962 when they recorded the worst record in MLB history. Also at that point they had their two tragic collapses in September in 2007 and 2008 as I discussed earlier in this book with Anthony, I held some hate. My editor wants me to clarify this part. It would be to mentally draining to Google it and then describe what happened exactly. Feel free to do it on your own. Just note it was bad. You invest so much time in loving a franchise and then they fall apart in front of your eyes. It causes some pain. I guess that's why fan is short for fanatical. I needed that book to always remind me to love my New York Mets.

There were other gifts that Georgianna and Cathie brought that day. I'm blanking on every gift I received. My guess is because of the importance of one gift. That gift was a David Wright T-shirt. The image was of David about to drop his bat as his body is fully twisted after completing his patented swing. I didn't cry. I did it once, before my spinal cord tumor surgery. Everyone gets one. (Family Guy) On the inside I was crying as they remembered my favorite athlete. That truly did mean a lot to me. I said, "Thank you" in my signature mumbled voice and I handed the shirt off to my mom as she folded it and put it back into the bag with the gifts.

My steak came and I ate it at the long pace I eat all food. Which as always annoyed me beyond belief even in this moment. My dad, who was closer to the waitress as she dropped the check, went to grab it. Georgianna put her hand out to stop him and paid for the meal. Before we left, I looked at these two people in amazement. One, they took time out of their night to come visit me when it came to picking my wish. Two, they got a reservation at Outback Steakhouse. Three, they bought gifts for me. Four, they paid for the entire meal. They were an impressive pair of people. Maybe one day I'll met them again.

The day finally came for my wish. My nurses, doctors, friends, and family members told me daily that I had been through a lot. Every time a new person told me that I would always nod my head up and down. I never really took the time to think about what the past four and half years were like for me. My first traumatic health concern; I woke up with an inability to walk. The second traumatic health concern; I woke up with an inability to identify my parents. My hope for this wish is it would allow me to put the past in the past.

   The morning of my wish, I woke up at 4:00 AM because a limo was scheduled to arrive in front of my house at 4:30. Yes, The Make-A-Wish Foundation gets a limo for every wish kid when they have a travel wish. Are you impressed? This was just the beginning.

I walked down the hallway to make sure my family was ready for the trip. It was like a child waking up Christmas morning and wanting to wake up their parents so they can open gifts. As I walked down the hallway, I looked at my brother's empty bedroom. He was unfortunately studying abroad in China. As I looked past my brother's bedroom, I looked at my parents, who were both already dressed and ready to go. My dad looked at me and joked, "You better get ready. The limo will leave without you."

I got ready and grabbed my David Wright t-shirt to wear all weekend. There was a lot of strength in that shirt, as it was official that David Wright would be the starting third baseman for the National League All-Stars. I thought it would be pretty cool to finally see my favorite athlete in person playing with other MLB All-Stars. To just view the game with him playing would be an incredible experience.

As the clock finally struck 4:30 AM, I walked down the stairs with my parents. I looked out the kitchen window and saw the limo pulling into the driveway. I immediately opened the garage and walked out to the limo with my parents.

My dad, who is a fan of talking with strangers, started to interact with the limo driver. "Hello there. We appreciate you picking us up on a Saturday morning." I walked behind my dad with my suitcase and overheard a response of, "Not a problem sir. We love doing work with The Make-A-Wish Foundation." At this point I started to think, who doesn't?

After all of the suitcases were put into the trunk, the limo driver opened my door as if I was as important as the players playing in the All-Star game. I stepped into the limo and found a seat, and for the first time, I started to smile thinking about the trip. I started to realize that for the next four days, I would have the ability to put the past in the past and just enjoy being me. For the next four days, there would be no worrying about MRIs or anything health related. For the first time in a while, all I had to worry about was being a normal teenager.

The limo parked in front of Bradley International Airport in Hartford. Although it was still dark outside of the car, I knew the day would eventually start to brighten up. I just couldn't figure out how the day would brighten. As soon as I started to think about it the limo driver opened the door and told me to enjoy my trip.

After a connecting flight, we arrived to a man holding up a sign that read 'Cory Metz' in the baggage claim area. I looked at this man and thought, well aren't we fancy? (The Eric Andre Show) Have you officially arrived in life if a complete stranger holds up a piece of paper with your name on it? I'll let you sleep on that question.

The three of us followed the limo driver to the limo and we were off to the hotel in the center of St. Louis, Missouri. As the limo moved for the 17-minute ride from the airport to the hotel, my excitement level was indescribable. I didn't talk with my parents. I just thought about what the future will hold.

Our limo pulled up in front of the Hotel Renaissance. Looking at it from the outside you could see it was a beautiful building, and it was just as beautiful inside. This hotel nailed the nice hotel checklist. Flowers, check, nice furniture, check, random person in the corner staring at me, check. Wait … what was the last one? I did a double-take and looked at this person as my parents went to the check-in area. She started walking toward us as if she knew us. My mom checked us in at the reception desk and as soon as the stranger heard the last name Metz, she walked closer and said, "Hello." As soon as she said it, I thought back to the itinerary and it mentioned someone from Make-A-Wish Missouri being in the lobby. The stranger was the person from Make-A-Wish Missouri. "Hello, I volunteer with the Missouri chapter, and I just wanted to welcome Cory to Missouri, and we hope he enjoys his stay here." Again, another act of kindness by the foundation and I've only been on this trip for six hours.

After checking in with the receptionist, the three of us found the elevator and traveled to our room in the Renaissance. The room was just as beautiful as the lobby. If I had to give a TripAdvisor review of the room, I would give it a five out of five. The reason being is that once I opened the door, I spotted the glass window that covered the entire wall, thus showcasing the entire city. It sat directly in front of me as to say, come and look at this city.

Two hours later we went back to the lobby and meet another representative from Make-A-Wish. At this point seven other 'wish' families were with us in the lobby. I did read on the itinerary that we would meet seven other wish families at this point in the schedule. Seeing the other seven wish families didn't upset me. I knew all seven of these other kids deserved their chance at a wish as much as I did, possibly more. All eight wish kids and wish families were told to follow the leader, and we walked to the ballroom inside the hotel. As we walked, I was the last wish kid in line. I noticed I was the only one who had issues with walking.

I looked around and walked toward the center of the room and saw the name tag Cory Metz on a table in the center of the ballroom. If you're keeping count that was the second name tag I saw today. If you have a highlighter on you be sure to highlight that. If you're using an e-reader, I wouldn't recommend you use a highlighter. If you're listening to this through speakers you shouldn't highlight your speakers either. I found a chair at the Cory Metz table with my mom and dad sitting beside me. I spotted a gift basket sitting directly in the center of the table. This caused me to jump up and grab the gift basket immediately like a child on their birthday. I looked at the gift basket and spotted a copy of MLB 2K9 for Xbox 360. Yes, I owned an Xbox 360. I'm old. This became my newest highlight of my trip. I loved seeing a copy of MLB 2K9 because the previous week I had rented a copy of MLB 2K9 from Blockbuster. Member' Blockbuster. (South Park) I took my copy of MLB 2K9 out of the basket and showed my mom as if I had an autographed baseball from my favorite player. I looked at my mom and said, "Hey, I just returned this game to Blockbuster a week ago and I really enjoyed it. I was planning on getting a copy for myself." My dad spotted a jersey on the table and handed to me. "See how it fits."

I looked at the jersey and thought about the last time I held a jersey. This caused me to think back to the spring of 2004. That spring I was just a normal thirteen year old. A boy who would never think he had any reason to write a memoir at the age of thirty. He was a boy who had great health and everything seemed to be working correctly for him. That boy would run onto the baseball diamond and enjoy the beautiful game of baseball that entire spring. Man, how I wish I had a time machine sometimes.

Now at eighteen, I was about to wear the same jersey the MLB All-Stars will wear in three days. I put the jersey on over my David Wright shirt, and being able to once again put a baseball jersey on was an incredible feeling.

As soon as the jersey went over my body it felt real. The 100% polyester felt like a warm blanket over my body on a wintery night. The only thing that could've been better would've been Gore-Tex.(Seinfeld) I looked on the table and spotted a wooden bat. I hadn't picked up a bat since the year 2004 as well. I grabbed the bat and got into the same batting stance I held since I was five years old. A stance my dad actually taught me. You hold the bat straight up with your right elbow pointing out, and then you lean your legs back and explode when the ball comes directly into the strike zone. It's a home run every time. Or at least I more than wished it was. Wait. You see I was trying to do the cliche thing they do in movies where they put the title of the movie into the movie. Did it work? The grammar was a little different though. I guess that wouldn't count.

I put my stance together and swung the bat like the baseball player I once was. In that moment my second wish was playing baseball in a regulation game. I guess you can never truly forget about the past.

After my strong cut with my new wooden bat, I took a seat and stared at the table sitting directly in front of me. Four empty chairs sat behind the long table. I looked at my parents and asked, "Who do you think will sit there?" They both looked at me and in unison shrugged their shoulders as this weekend was as much a surprise to them as it was to me. I thought maybe David Wright would sit there.

All of a sudden, four people walked into the room. All eight tables of wish families turned and watched these four bodies walk in expecting them to pull off some sort of a magic act in front of all of us. Maybe they would. This had been a magical day so far.

All four bodies took a seat and looked at the eight tables. The man all the way to the right spoke up at first. He didn't look like a baseball player. "Hello kids. I work with the MLB and I am here to welcome you to your Make-A-Wish weekend. We have a lot planned for all of you during this event. With me are three players playing in the future games."

All three of the players spoke eloquently about being at the game and all three mentioned how it was an honor to speak in front of us. That was nice to hear as the honors were clearly going both ways.

The speeches ended and all of a sudden, the youngest kid in our group walked over to the players with his baseball bat. All of the players smiled and signed the bat. The players were kind enough to repeat this process seven more times.

After every wish kid had interacted with the three MLB future players, the representative from the MLB asked, "Do you kids want to go to Busch Stadium, today?"

At this point in my life I had only visited Shea Stadium, Yankee Stadium for the 2008 Home Run Derby, and Citi Field. I didn't research what Busch Stadium looked like before my trip. The stadium had been built in 2006, so I imagined it was beautiful.

We followed the MLB representative to a bus sitting in front of the hotel. My parents took a seat in front of me and we were off. The three MLB stadiums I had already visited were beautifully built stadiums. I don't know if you can understand this or not, but being in New England all winter, especially a snowy winter, where I had to sleep in a hospital bed for the majority of it, caused my excitement to grow as the bus traveled. I knew seeing Busch Stadium would improve my mood. The bus traveled a little further and before I knew it, I was in front of Busch Stadium. Looking up I thought this stadium would prove if the next four days are really a success in providing a life-changing wish.

The MLB representative went to the side entrance of the stadium and told us to follow him. We followed him into the stadium and walked toward the diamond. You can smell the fresh-cut grass (Happy Gilmore) and the feeling of America's pastime just run through your body. There were no birds chirping though. The feeling I had was something you couldn't explain. Although as an author I probably should.

We walked to the backstop and looked out toward center field. I assumed the MLB representative would just show us the field from the stands. But instead, he opened the mini gate that protects the fans from the players and asked, "Do you want to follow me?" I looked at him and thought, me walk back onto a baseball field? The last time I did that was in my hometown in 2004. At that field, the majority of fans sat in folding chairs that parents brought from their cars. Busch stadium sat a capacity crowd of 45,538 people. I guess you could say stepping on an MLB field was a bit of an upgrade.

The MLB representative opened up the moveable fence, and I took a step onto the field. I thought that this is what the moon landing must have felt like. The feeling of your feet touching something you've never felt before. That's one small step for man and another giant leap for a boy who at one point thought he would never walk again.

We started our tour by walking into the dugout along the first-base line. All eight families walked straight into the dugout together, and I saw every kid had the imagination of being an MLB player. All eight of us either stood over the fence acting as if we were watching a ninth- inning rally or sat on the bench and stared directly at the pitcher's mound. It was fun to see all eight of the wish kids put their health in the past in that one moment.

For me, my mind went to the greatest moment in baseball. I sat on the bench and imagined I was witnessing the seventh game of the World Series. Although no MLB players were on the field at that moment, I could picture it. The count is 3-2 bottom of the ninth with two outs. My team is up by one run. The pitcher throws a 3-2 fastball past the batter and strikes the hitter out. We did it! We just won the World Series! The trophy we had been working for all season was now ours. In this scenario I didn't walk with a limp. I didn't have a brain shunt. I didn't have issues with eating. I was an MLB baseball player who worked hard enough to get to the majors, and I ran on the field to celebrate the World Series. Maybe in a different world.

The seven other wish families exited the dugout, while I was still stuck thinking about being an MLB superstar. My mom had to come and tell me it was time to go. Oh yeah, this wasn't the local field I played on during elementary school and middle school. The number of chairs in the outfield was the dead giveaway. There clearly wasn't a shortage. (Family Guy)

I took one step out of the dugout without a batting helmet, unfortunately, and walked around the entire field with my parents. We passed the first-base line and I noticed the height of the stadium walls. I started to see how they were much larger in person. As a kid you look at these walls on television and you think it's nothing, I could scale them and grab a ball easily. I put my hand on the wall and felt the soft padding. It had a very comfortable feel. Let's just say it didn't feel like the chain-linked fences I was used to. I imagined Albert Pujols hitting a high fly ball to the right field and in that moment, I would catch it. Catching a fly ball is all about timing. Keep in mind, I didn't have the pressure of 45,538 people looking at me and the millions of fans watching at home during this simulation. Maybe it's not as easy as it seems.

We walked by the bullpen. The bullpen is where MLB pitchers warm up before they pitch. The hope is you warm up enough and then you can run from the bullpen to the mound. My bullpens were hospitals and rehab centers. At this point in my life, my stays in these facilities combined had been around four months. I needed these facilities to help warm my body up to a point where I could function in front of others. Just like the pitcher coming out from the bullpen.

I continued to walk on the dirt along the outfield edge looking at home plate, marveling at how large this stadium is. If you have the chance to ever tour a local baseball stadium, I suggest you take it. There's only so much a fan can take away from his television screen, or sitting in the stands while watching a baseball game.

We finally made it back to home plate, and I took it all in for one final time. I thought, just imagine 45,538 screaming fans as I approach home plate. The pitcher standing sixty feet and six inches away, planning his best way to force me to swing and miss at three pitches. It's one of the greatest head-to-head match-ups in sports. Every time a hitter steps into the batter's box, he has to strategize and think, what will this pitcher do against me? Will he throw a 95-mph fastball or will he fool me with a 75-mph curveball? The pitcher can also throw the ball outside the strike zone and fool the hitter into swinging the bat. It's one of the greatest cat and mouse games in sports. We arrived back at the hotel, and I went to bed imagining what tomorrow would be like.

The second day of my wish trip came and I read the itinerary. It stated the Futures game and the celebrity softball game would be today. I didn't have any idea who was playing in either game. I was just here for the All-Star game after all.

All eight of us arrived at Busch Stadium, but this time it was raining. That kind of put a damper on the day at first. I thought this was supposed to be a perfect weekend and the weather would corporate with the theme of perfection. Nothing bad should happen during my trip.

This time a different MLB representative brought us to our seats in Busch Stadium. Yesterday we were just introduced to the stadium with a tour and we hadn't been told where we were sitting. I honestly didn't care where they put us at this point. I just wanted to watch America's pastime being played by the greatest baseball players in the world. Where the seats were in the stadium didn't matter to me. We were brought to the Albert Pujols suite! All eight of us walked in the suite and looked at it in amazement. I looked around and it was as decorative as you could imagine. The suite had a bar and a table that was continually getting filled with food.

That meant nothing to me. I walked away from the bar and walked to our seats. The seats are the only thing I was interested in. There were twelve seats attached to the suite looking at Busch Stadium. They had to be the best seats in the house. Thank you, MLB.

The rain stopped and baseball players ran onto the field and started to warm up. Seeing that I sat further up in my chair still waiting for the game to begin. Then I heard someone yell, "Cory, come here."

I was just about to relax. What could anyone possibly want? I stood up and walked toward the MLB representative. She talked to all eight of us and told us she had a surprise for us outside of the suite. She said, "Do you guys want to follow me?"

We followed her as she continued taking us downstairs floor by floor in Busch Stadium. Eventually, we got down to the basement. Because of all of this walking, I started to get tired. I'll let you in on a little secret. Busch Stadium is a building that cost 365 million dollars to build. But no matter how expensive a building is a basement is still a basement. The basement was incredibly dark with narrow hallways that two full-grown bodies couldn't walk side-by-side through. I was waiting for a spider to fall on my head at one point because the basement was so creepy and old looking.

We made it to the end of the hall and the MLB representative stopped all eight of us and told us to stand where we were. She took a few steps forward and walked into a mystery room.

I wanted to break from the line and have a first peak at what was behind the mystery door. Was it a brand-new car? I started to hear a few voices talking amongst each other in the mystery room, so it couldn't be a new car. Unless they were the cars from the movie Cars. Lighting McQueen. You know what, maybe… (The Dan Le Batard Show)

After about ten seconds she came back out and waved all eight of us together to walk into the mystery room.

The mystery room was a bar with a bunch of random people I didn't recognize. Naturally being in Busch Stadium, there were Budweiser and Busch fluorescent lights on the three walls keeping the room well lit. All eight of us stood in a corner as if it was a middle school dance and we were all afraid to be the first one on the dance floor. Naturally the youngest wish kid, who was probably around eight years old, who had developed a shiner after getting hit with a baseball during one of his little league games, started walking toward the random people. I chuckled to myself and thought he had youth on his side and a story with his shiner. He had yet to develop an awkward phase and couldn't grasp the concept of looking like a fool in front of others just yet. To be young again. (Knocked Up) I wasn't planning on starting a conversation with these random people.

The number of wish kids standing in the corner playing with their thumbs and waiting for this random event to end started to dwindle. One kid went over and talked to a short girl, another went over to the guy with white hair. I kept looking around and thinking, what are these kids doing? Didn't they know these people weren't the MLB All-Stars? Who cares about them?

Then all of a sudden, I looked to the left of me and I recognized one of the random people. I elbowed the kid next to me with such force you would've thought the President of the United States was in the room. Luckily this wish kid didn't break rank and I could talk to him, I asked, "Is that Andy Richter?"

He looked back at me and shrugged his shoulders as if to say, "Who the hell is Andy Richter?" Also, I could tell he was thinking, you better never elbow me again.

Just in case you forgot while I was in the hospital I would occasionally sleep during the day or because I didn't have to worry about waking up for school in the morning, I would train myself to stay up till 12:37 AM.

Why you ask? Because at 12:37 AM Late Night with Conan O'Brien was on NBC. On June 1st of that year, Conan O'Brien moved from 12:37 AM to 11:35 PM and became the host of The Tonight Show with Conan O'Brien, and Andy Richter was back as his sidekick. I hadn't missed one episode of the new Tonight Show with Conan O'Brien. I even recorded the show with my DVR in case I feel asleep. I had to break rank and go talk with Andy Richter.

I took my own marching orders and took a couple of steps to the left and stood diagonally across from Andy. He was having a conversation with another person who I had now assumed was a celebrity. I didn't want to barge right in and yell, "Mr. Richter can I have an autograph?" Andy Richter held his conversation for about ten seconds and the random celebrity pointed at me and he said, "Looks like he wants to talk to you." Andy Richter turned and said, "Hi there." I didn't speak at first. This was my first celebrity encounter ever. I had to wonder, do celebrities use the same language as us in their private lives? Are they the same as "average" people? I had my autograph pad from Make-A-Wish on me, and I put it directly in front of Andy Richter without saying anything. He looked at me and asked, "Do you want me to sign that?" I was doing it, this was happening. I was talking with a celebrity. Something the everyday folk only dream about. Oh wait, I hadn't said anything yet. I looked up and said, "Yes." Andy grabbed my pen and pad and searched for a page to write on. As he searched for a page, I had the courage to open up to this man I didn't even know. I told him that I loved the fact he was back on the Tonight Show, and I loved the bits they were doing in the new time slot and told him to keep up the good work. It's funny because I saw two different psychiatrists after both of my major surgeries, because what I went through was considered life-altering. And I'm not ashamed to admit this: I was more open with Andy Richter compared to my two therapists. Is that a good thing or bad thing? Who knows, I'm not a doctor. Andy Richter found an open page and signed his name and thanked me. He also, wrote "Thank's above his autograph. That meant a lot knowing he valued my opinion. I mean with me in his corner, The Tonight Show with Conan O'Brien should go on forever.

Unfortunately, nine months later, the show would be cancelled. I guess my opinion isn't as valuable as I thought.

As I continued to look around the room, I grabbed a few more autographs and all of a sudden I spotted Billy Bob Thornton with an elbow on the make shift bar in the corner of this random room in the basement of Busch Stadium. I was on a high after what I believed to be a long conversation with Andy Richter. I knew I could handle a conversation with Billy Bob Thornton or at least I thought I could.

I walked toward the bar and stared at Billy Bob Thornton. All of the sudden I realized I'm not good at … wait let me think about it. Words. It had to be at least ten seconds until he turned around as he was holding a conversation with another celebrity and asked, "Do you want me to sign that?" I didn't utter any words; I just held my pad like some kind of caveman and expected some kind of reaction. Billy Bob took my pad with glee and asked, "What's your name?" I had to admit that I had a tough time maintaining eye contact while in the presence of greatness. This was the man who did an incredible job playing Bad Santa. I looked at Bad Santa and said, "Cory." He looked at me and respectfully said, "What?"

The noise in the room were a little loud as the celebrities in the game were still commiserating amongst each other. The inside voice I use on a daily basis needed to be elevated. I didn't want to disappoint Bad Santa.

I raised my voice a little and said," Cory." Mr. Woodcock looked at me once again and yelled in the proper voice in a crowded room, "Gordon?" At this point, I honestly thought he was joking. Although I tend to be on the quieter side, so who am I to blame Woodcock? I feel like if I did blame him, he would've told me to take a lap. (Mr. Woodcock)

This was my last attempt. I took a deep breath in and said, "Cory!" in my loudest voice possible and Mr. Thornton signed his name into my autographed pad. I was happy with all my autographs and I couldn't wait to go back to my seat to look at all of them. Wait, I failed to mention the man Billy Bob Thornton was talking to at the makeshift bar..... Bob Knight. Can you think of a more intimidating actor and iconic sports figure combination? Mr. Knight was kind enough to sign the autograph pad too without saying anything. He kind of just gave me a grunt and took my autograph pad. My celebrity meet and greet ended.

I found my seat in the Albert Pujols suite and looked through my autographs like a kid opening his first set of baseball cards.

There's Andy Richter, Jon Hamm, Carl Edwards, Shawn Johnson. And finally, Billy Bob Thornton. It reads, "To Gordon, signed Billy Bob Thornton."

After my failed celebrity encounter, I watched the rest of the Futures game and celebrity softball game with my parents and the other wish families. Although the weather didn't cooperate that day, I still had fun, and I was looking forward to the Home Run Derby tomorrow. Maybe I'll finally meet David Wright.

The next morning, I ate breakfast and played the scenario in my head. David Wright stands in front of me. I tell him my name, where I am from, how he's my favorite player and that I love the way he plays third base with reckless abandonment. As breakfast came to an end, the MLB representative told families and friends to go explore the city while the Make-A-Wish children will follow her.

I waved to my parents and followed her to her surprise. We went further into the ballroom, and all of a sudden I spotted television personalities. I looked in wonderment as I could've sworn that I saw Peter Gammons just hanging out and having a conversation. It was odd and I had to wonder, why was he here? The MLB representative opened the door to this random room and brought us into an area with what seemed like a million cameras, and she found us seats to sit in.

Once I sat down, I looked at who these cameras were for. I saw Joe Maddon, Roy Holliday, Charlie Manuel, and Tim Lincecum sitting at the front of the ballroom. We were sitting at the 2009 MLB All-Star press conference! I was amazed as I always admired the world of sports journalism as a kid and couldn't believe I was at a real press conference.

Eventually the MLB representative grabbed us and told us we have more in store. Before we left I stood up and grabbed a microphone. I then yelled, "baba booey baba booey baba booey." (Howard Stern) Legally that didn't actually happen. I just wanted to connect Howard Stern to my wish trip in some way, since meeting him was my first idea.

We followed the MLB representative to a new room inside the hotel. This room was the size of an elementary school classroom. I looked around and thought, this room isn't anything special and why am I here?

I started to observe the MLB representative, and a Make-A-Wish representative started unrolling some kind of banner. I read the banner and it said Make-A-Wish on the front. The organization that brought all of this together. I knew I could I never repay the Foundation for what they've done for me so far. Maybe one day I'll try to do my best.

Once the banner was undone, within seconds I spotted Albert Pujols and Ryan Howard walking down the hallway. I looked and thought they must be going somewhere else to some type of press conference. Instead, they walked into our room and started to have conversations with every wish kid. Before they came to me, I started to think, what do I say? This is the moment every boy dreams of, an opportunity to be in front of a professional athlete.

I scrambled to find the baseball my mom told me to bring in case I was getting autographs today. Luckily Pujols and Howard hadn't left the room by the time I found a ball. Howard stood in front of me and signed my baseball. The same process occurred with Pujols. I know I should probably put some dialogue here. There was none. I stopped and stared as I got both autographs. I hope you've learned by now that celebrity encounters aren't as easy as they seem. This same interaction would occur with every new MLB player walking into the room. Adrian Gonzalez, Ichiro Suzuki, Adam Jones, etc. Then, he came into the room.

"Now walking into the room, number two, Derek Jeter, number two." (Legendary Bob Sheppard voice) This was the man who caused me so many problems growing up as a Mets fan in Yankees country. In case you're too young to remember, Derek Jeter was the captain of the New York Yankees and the greatest reason the Yankees dynasty existed from 1996 through 2009. I just happened to start kindergarten in 1996. He was the reason I had to walk into school after a Yankees World Series victory and hear my friends brag about winning another World Series. I still hadn't gotten past the year 2000, when the Yankees beat the Mets in the Subway Series.

Before we go any further, I have my own 'In the Year 2000' joke. That was a bit on Late Night With Conan O'Brien.

'Tired of being the younger brother to the New York Yankees, the New York Mets will relocate to a ballpark on Mars in the hopes of easily winning a championship against aliens. They will still manage to lose the championship as they will compete against aliens who use performance-enhancing drugs." I'll await a call from the Conan writing staff.

If the younger version of myself knew I would be face-to-face with Derek Jeter, he would want me to confront him. I can hear him in my mind yelling, come on Cory, this man caused every Yankees fan to brag about how great their team was. I stared the enemy down as he just walked away from a different wish child, and he was coming my way.

The enemy said, "Hi, there." Is that how enemies greet each other? I don't know, I've never had a reason to make enemies with anyone before. I looked at him and thought that those were fighting words. I responded, "Hello." And the battle was on. We stared at each other with strong discontent and almost came to blows. He looked at the baseball in my hand and asked, "Would you like me to sign that?" No, don't do it. He's the enemy, did you forget that?

I handed him the ball. As he signed the ball he looked up and saw my New York Mets hat and asked, "Are you a New York Mets fan?" And to continually disappoint every Derek Jeter hater I responded, "Yes I am." As he signed the ball he said, "That's great, good luck in your future." I took the baseball and said, "Thank you." To every Derek Jeter hater on earth. I'm sorry for failing you.

More players continued to walk in: Joe Mauer, Josh Hamilton, and Jason Bay. I was happy to get every autograph as players continually walked in. These were the players I admired on television as I would watch their highlights as a kid and teenager, and now they're inches away from me.

Eventually there came a point where the fun had to end, and players stopped walking into the room. And now the Make-A-Wish banner was being taken down by the Make-A-Wish rep and the MLB rep.

David Wright never showed up. I'd be a liar if I told you that I wasn't a little upset. He was my favorite player, and I watched the seven other kids get to meet their favorite players. The Yankees fans got to meet Derek Jeter. The Red Sox fans got to meet Kevin Youkilis. The Twins fan got to meet Joe Mauer. How come I didn't get to meet my favorite player?

Once everything was packed up, all eight of us went back to FanFest, and I spotted my parents as we walked through the building. I broke off and hung out with them for the rest of the day. They both asked, "How was your day?" I replied as if I was keeping a secret. It was good. We walked around the exhibits at Fanfest, which took place in the St. Louis convention center for a couple of hours and went back to the hotel room.

I showed my parents all of the autographs I received. They both looked in amazement and my mom asked, "How was meeting David Wright?" She assumed that David Wright had shown up to this event as I had autographs from every player playing in the game. "He didn't show up." My mom looked back in anger and replied, "What?" It was one of those voices I recognized where I thought I had made a mistake. I looked back at her and simply said, "He must've been busy." I appreciated her concern, but I've learned in life you have to be happy with what you have. I was happy with getting a ton of autographs from other players. I thought that it's okay and let's just move forward with our lives.

All eight families met in the lobby once again before the Home Run Derby, and I spotted the MLB rep who was helping Make-A-Wish standing in the lobby looking at me. As she stared at me, she pointed her finger at me and moved it toward her indicating I needed to talk to her. It felt like the principal coming into your classroom and calling you out in front of the other students. I walked over.

"Hi Cory, I tried to get David Wright to the autograph session, but he had a prior media engagement he was obligated to attend." I looked at her and thought, I almost confronted Derek Jeter today. It's alright, It's not the end of the world. I'm sure you did the best you could. I replied, "It's okay."

We went to Busch Stadium and watched the Home Run Derby together and Prince Fielder would end up winning the contest. Back at the hotel I went to bed knowing the final surprise of this weekend would be watching the All-Star game and that's it. I couldn't wait to watch all of the All-Stars play together in this one event.

After the Derby, families were told they could go the Gateway Arch or sleep in the next morning. I thought it would be nice to sleep in for one day. My dad looked at me and said, "We're going. The Gateway Arch is a historic sight."

We woke up at 7:30 and meet in the lobby. I couldn't wait to go visit the Gateway Arch. As a kid I would watch games where the St. Louis Rams or the St. Louis Cardinals would play football, and the arch would be shown after a commercial break. It didn't seem that large on television.

The bus pulled in front of the Arch and I was stunned. Maybe it was because I've always been height deficient or the fact that the arch is 630' feet tall? Looking up at the arch was a daunting task. Do you remember being a little kid and looking up at a tall adult and thinking, how can that person be so tall? Well the Gateway Arch is just like that. Just imagine playing Jenga with 105 adults who were six feet tall, and you would reach the top of the Gateway Arch. How's that for height?

I followed the group and we walked into an entrance near the front of the Arch. As we walked, I looked and saw we were in a museum. Looking at this museum you could see it was very well built as it told the story of the Midwest, a world I had only read about in history books in school.

After looking at some of the exhibits, my parents and I followed the group to a tunnel. Our group leader then gave us tickets. I grabbed my ticket with some minor hesitation wondering where we were going. Are we going deeper into to the museum? I guess maybe the part of the museum that requires a ticket.

We walked to a room with eight doors. As I looked at all eight of the doors it felt like a game of Let's Make A Deal. We stood by door number eight and waited for something to happen. All of a sudden all the doors opened and people came out of tiny pods behind each door. I bet you get that a lot on Let's Make A Deal. (Happy Gilmore)

As I approached the doors I noticed we were about to step into tiny pods. To say the pods inside the St. Louis Arch are small would be an understatement. The pods are really only built for one person to fit in. The three of us stepped in the pod and traveled up the Arch. Traveling up a pod in the Arch isn't for the claustrophobic. The three of us are each five feet and five inches tall, and we needed to lean in a little as the pod traveled to the top of the Arch. Imagine three Shaquille O'Neal's in those pods, I don't think it's possible to get one.

We arrived at the top and followed the crowd to the left. All of the sudden the crowd started to stop at the top of the stairs as we started to walk and they seemed to be looking at something together.

I arrived at the top of the steps and noticed kids and adults looking out windows. We were at the top of the Gateway Arch. Do you guys want to hear about The Gateway Arch? It was indescribable. (The Office)

Before the All-Star game the MLB puts on a red-carpet parade for all of the MLB All-Stars. The players come from their hotel in Chevy pick-up trucks and enter the stadium. It's a time for the fans to line up and see their heroes enter the stadium.

The MLB set up stands for wish kids and families right in front of the entrance to the stadium. I was amazed by how generous that was considering our family and friends didn't get a chance to meet the players, yet. Everyone went to the stands and waited for the players to walk by. Some players waved as they walked in. Other players stopped and spent time giving autographs to siblings of wish children. My enemy Derek Jeter came by and signed autographs. The MLB representative stood next to me with a walkie talkie and continually looked at me. Eventually she said, "Get ready in a minute or two." I looked at her and wondered what that meant as she walked away and stood next to where the Chevy pickup trucks were parking as the players would walk into the stadium. I looked up at the next truck and it said 'David Wright' on it. I began to smile and thought he's here, he's here. He'll walk by us and I'll finally get to wave hello. The MLB representative had a different idea, and she waved to me indicating she wanted me to stand near her as David Wright got off the truck. No wish kid did this the entire morning. I looked at my mom and dad with a nervous curiosity wondering if it was okay to walk over. They both looked at me and waved their hands toward David Wright as if to say, 'This is your moment; go and take it.' My mom was also smart enough to give me a pen in that moment. I took a large breath and took a few steps over to the truck. David Wright was still waving to the crowd as I finally stopped near the truck. The MLB rep told me to stand there as she would go talk with David Wright first and tell him my story. My body started to shake with anticipation, as I was only a couple feet away from David Wright.

The MLB representative started to talk with David Wright, and I started to think about what I would say. I knew I failed on numerous occasions previously when it came to talking with celebrities and athletes. This time I wouldn't fail. "Hello Mr. Wright, it's an honor to meet you. You've been my favorite athlete ever since you've entered the majors. I admire the way you play the hot corner." It'll be something like that.

The conversation with the MLB representative and David Wright ended and she waved me over to come and talk with him.

I tried my best to make my leg muscles power forward. This was my moment. I could feel it in my bones. I stood in front of David Wright and stared at him just like I did with every celebrity/athlete interaction. Again meeting people you see on television is a lot tougher than you can imagine. Luckily, David Wright was kind enough to start. "Hi. I want to apologize for not seeing you yesterday. I had a media obligation during that time. It's very nice to meet you." I still didn't move my mouth and verbalize a response. I wish I had said, "That's okay, your apology is completely unnecessary, I do appreciate it though." You know the type of a response a normal human being would make. Instead, I held my hat out and expected David Wright to pick up on the fact I wanted him to sign my hat. He did and asked, "Do you want me to sign that?" I looked at him and nodded.

The MLB representative smiled and said, "How about a picture?" She told me to move in more, and I was now shoulder-to-shoulder with my hero. The picture was taken and we shook hands. I said, "Thank you." At least I had enough respect to remember that part. I was the only wish kid who got to meet their favorite player separately and take a photo individually that day. It was the greatest moment of my life at that point.

All of the MLB players ended up walking by us and into Busch Stadium. Staff members were rolling the red carpet up, and that was our cue to leave and enter the stadium with the players. All eight of us wish kids and their friends and families walked into the same entrance. Our wish experience was complete. Before I walked into the stadium, I thought about what this moment meant to me. This time I wasn't walking into a hospital, a rehabilitation center, or a physician's office and being told I had to have surgery or a procedure. This was my greatest entrance, as I was walking into Busch Stadium and completing my dream wish.

All of us walked to our seats in the Albert Pujols suite for one final time and waited for the All-Star game to begin. At this point we were about eight hours early, as the red carpet ended at twelve.

The MLB representative talked to all eight of us wish kids for a final time and said, "Do you boys want to meet Barack Obama?" I was just waiting for the MLB All-Star game to start at this point. To meet a sitting president will be something for sure. We followed her downstairs once again. This time she led us to a different basement in the stadium. I would describe the placement of this room like a bomb shelter inside Busch Stadium. It sat directly underneath the seats behind home plate. The MLB representative knocked on the door. The door was opened and a man peaked at all nine of us and said, "How can I help you?" She said, "Hi, I'm with the children from The Make-A-Wish Foundation." The man from behind the door said, "Hi, he's not here yet." The MLB representative took all eight of us back up the stairs. As we waited, all eight of us looked around with a strange curiosity wondering what it will be like to meet a sitting president. We followed the MLB representative as she walked down the stairs once again and asked, "Can these kids come into the room?" The person behind the door looked at her once again and said it was fine this time.

We all walked into the room and for national security purposes, I will just say it was beautiful room. All eight of us found seats and waited for Barack Obama to walk in. I hope I'm not breaking any laws by describing any of this.

A few minutes had gone by and all of a sudden, Barack Obama entered the room. If you've never met Barack Obama before, he has a way of commanding the room. Immediately he came over and shook every child's hand and asked for our names and where we were from. He also handed every child a special presidential coin. This was the perfect ending to my wish. Just as going up The Gateway Arch is indescribable so is meeting a sitting president. Sounds awesome. (The Office)

15

Now that my wish was over it was time for college. College. (Around the Horn) College is an eight-letter word that equals excellence. For you grammar experts, yes I'm in on the joke. ;)

Anyway for me college was a different experience. What made it tough for me was I now had to learn new things while living with a brain tumor. Before the brain tumor I wasn't James Holzhauer from Jeopardy, but I was quick. I wrote that joke on May 25, 2019. I hope James Holzhauer references are still being made by the time this book is published. If not feel free to Google him. The man is a genius. My greatest attribute was my ability to remember names. If you told me your name once, I would remember your name 30 days later. I would actually get upset with people who would forget my name after meeting me once. Now if someone came up to me and told me their name, I would hear it once, and as if it was some cartoon, the name would go through my right ear past my brain then through my left ear and onto the floor. It was as if our conversation had never happened. A name has to be told to me multiple times for me to truly remember it.

Because of this I got into the disability resource center at Southern Connecticut State University. Being in the disability resource center as a freshman, I was offered a chance at the suites in West Campus at Southern.

They call suites, 'suite,' because they are sweet. I'm not a grammar expert remember. My suite was a prime example as it had four individual bedrooms, two bathrooms, and one living room. Although I wasn't staying at the Ritz-Carlton or whatever fancy hotel you can name, this bedroom felt just as nice as any hotel you could name because it was my room. My television was put on top of my dresser with my Xbox 360. My new clothes were put into the dressers provided to me. Sheets were put on the bed, and I was officially a student at Southern Connecticut State University.

I thanked my mom and dad for helping with my setting up my room. I gave them a hug and they both told me, "If you need anything or if anything happens with your health, you call us. One of us will be here." I appreciated the offer of help, but I was a college student now. I don't need help from outsiders anymore. I only take help from people in college.

My first class in college was a morning course and the subject has escaped my mind. The subject of course didn't matter; it was the fact I was there. It was eight months ago when I woke up with zero memory of my past life. I worked up to a point where I could attend a university and that meant something.

After my first class, I walked through the university to find the disability resource center. I wanted to walk over and thank them for the suite. I found the room on the first floor of Engleman Hall. As soon as I opened the door, I realized something: I have no idea who to talk with. I'm going to thank someone who I don't even know. I spotted the reception desk and said, "Hi, I wanted to thank the person who got me into the suite." With good reason the person at the reception desk stared at me as if I had two heads. "Excuse me?" I became nervous wondering if I was in the wrong disability resource center. How many students could have disabilities if there's a need for two resource centers? I'm new to having a learning disability, so maybe there's a need for two disability resource centers. How would I know?

I nervously said a response, "I have a learning disability and a walking disability, and I was given a suite at West Campus. I just wanted to thank the person who got me the suite." Looking at her face, I could still tell the person behind the desk was still confused by what I wanted exactly, but just to get me to leave she came up with a response. "Okay, Deb Fairchild is the head of the disability resource center, do you want to set up appointments with her? That made the most sense. It took a while, but I'm glad we figured it out and I made an appointment.

Meeting with Deb Fairchild was a good experience. This is true for anyone whether you have a disability, if you are going through something traumatic, or have gone through something traumatic, always talk to someone. I saw therapists after I came back from the spinal cord tumor and brain tumor. I would sit there and not say much during our meetings. If you haven't learned by now, I'm not a very talkative person. Opening up to anyone, let alone this random person sitting in an office holding a clipboard, seemed like nonsense our first few sessions. Although I didn't get it at first by the end of our sessions, I started to confess my feelings and left with positive feelings on what therapy means.

After the brain tumor, I went to a different therapist, and this time I came prepared and wrote a page full of notes. The notes ended up being so impressive; I actually caused my therapist to stare at me in shock for a few seconds. She told me, "Wow no one has ever been this prepared for therapy." She actually cried during the session. Don't keep your feelings trapped inside of you. Talk to others whether that is a therapist or a friend.

I talked with Deb and she said, "You're welcome for the room. May I recommend something for you? Actually may I recommend two things for you? One is that we have a club for students with disabilities called Outreach Unlimited. I like to think of it as a social gathering for students with disabilities. Two is weekly meetings with me. I won't pressure you into them, but I think they will help." Always willing to try things once when suggested, I agreed to her two meetings.

Walking into the first meeting at Outreach Unlimited was an entirely new experience. I spotted students in wheelchairs. Students who started to speak to me who clearly had a verbal disabilities. Some disabilities you couldn't see as they were seated, but once they stood up to walk you knew they had one. Just like me, at least for one of my disabilities.

Introductions started and we were told to say our name, year, and disability if we wanted to talk about our disability. It was an option as some people may not be comfortable with it. Knowing I had the option I just stated my name and my year.

 The meeting went by with discussions about raising disability awareness and that was about all I could remember. It seemed boring and unimportant to me. Does disability awareness need to be raised? I used to not have a disability, and me being aware of disability didn't do much for my life. For the rest of the year, I wouldn't go to another meeting. The club didn't really appeal to me.

The same lack of appeal came with my meetings with Deb Fairchild. Some meetings I would show up, and others I wouldn't bother. Talking about or caring about my disability wasn't something I wanted to do, at least not in public.

What I did do my entire freshman year was live a life of loneliness. It was a repeat of my four years at Fairfield Prep. I would go to the library every night to just study the work given by professors that day. Then go to Conn Hall to attempt to eat the food there. I'm strictly speaking about my issues with Crohn's disease and in no way talking bad about the food served at Conn Hall. Then play NHL '09 on my television and then sleep. I was nowhere close to the big man on campus.

By sophomore year I still went to the DRC to get accommodations for my disability and Deb stopped me before I could slither out of the room like a snake. "Hey Cory, I want you to give me one more meeting this year, if it doesn't work, you'll never have to meet again." I nodded and gave into meeting one more time. Cory Metz always does stuff twice. Is that hypocritical, after my earlier statement? Who's keeping up? I walked into her office for what I hoped would be the final time as I realized I'm terrible at saying 'no' to people. I took my seat in Deb's office and she stared at me.

"How's everything going?"

This was starting to turn into any lie detector scene you see in any television show or movie that you can think of.

"It's going well," I said with a lack of confidence.

If you never meet me in person, I'll tell you one secret about me or really lack of a secret to the ones who know me. I'm a terrible liar. If you have a secret, I prefer you never tell me.

Deb spotted this and told me, "Alright come to one more Outreach Unlimited meeting. If you truly embrace the people in the club, I think you'll enjoy it."

I gave in and went to the next meeting with the same hesitation as I did before of not wanting to open up about my disability. An open mind never came with my disability.

Walking or limping, however you want to define it, into another Outreach Unlimited meeting was a little different. As a few faces disappeared and new faces entered. I still wasn't talking about my disability in the meeting, but a new face named Heather Walton was leading the meeting. She led the meetings with a fun attitude, and I started to see the importance of the meetings and communicating with people who had disabilities.

I took an acting class in college as well. It was a last semester elective, and my advisor recommended it. Electives are meant to be fun classes. I thought maybe acting could be fun.

Not to get all high and mighty on you, but have you ever acted before? How Nicolas Cage does this form of art in every movie amazes me. Acting is very tough. "Not the bees. Not the bees." (The Wicker Man)

I walked into the Lyman Center, which as a kid I had visited for shows while in elementary school. It's funny to think about how as a little kid, the Lyman Center looked so scary and big to me, and now it's just a small venue that fits 1,500. I was looking forward to acting on the stage I once viewed as a kid. It's funny how things work out. Have you begun to pick up on that? By the way, how was your day today? I've been reading a lot of memoirs to help me understand the best way to craft a perfect memoir. I've noticed none of them ask, "How are you doing? I hope you're doing well. Also, don't forget to get your eight hours of sleep in. I would hate for you to be cranky tomorrow." I'll explain why I've read so many books a little later.

Our first class didn't take place in front of a sold-out Lyman Center. Which was probably safer for someone who's never acted before. Although, Tommy Wiseau never acted in anything major before in his life, and he was able to make a great movie. "Oh, hi Mark." (The Room)

The first class took place directly behind the stage. My first break wasn't meant to happen just yet. It wasn't a classroom with desks. It was set up like a ballet studio. It was just one giant room. I guess us actors need our room to perform.

I found seats in the corner of the room and buried myself in the corner, and even though the class hadn't started I felt out of place. I held the thought of, how am I going to do well in acting class, when I've never attempted it before?

Professor Rarick walked in and told everyone to gather in front of her. I had a feeling it was her way of calling out the student who buried himself sitting in the corner. I obliged and moved toward the professor with a little less fear, as she didn't seem scary to me. I had never been to an acting class before, but I imagine like anything there's good and bad instructors. She didn't seem like a bad one.

She looked at us and seemed happy to have students in her class. Which only further cemented my feeling of knowing she was a good teacher. She went around asking for every student's name and why they were here. A majority of the students said their name and said they were theater majors, which is typically what happens in classes. Next up was my introduction.

I told the class that I wasn't a theater major (the only person in class who wasn't), and I just wanted to take an elective that was different and interested me. Looking at the course catalogue, this class fit the bill.

Everyone mentioned their reason for being there, and we were ready to learn. After my statement not much happened, which is typical on the first day of most classes. It was student introductions and looking at the rubric for the entire semester. I spotted one thing and one thing only on that rubric: your self-portrait.

I had my assumptions on what that meant exactly. I imagined it wasn't anything good for me. To give a true self-portrait of my life? I'll make a strong pass.

Walking into class I had little scribble notes of a few jokes about myself. I didn't want to be really serious as I've never been comfortable with that. I also wrote about how I had a spinal cord tumor and then brain tumor cells showed up. It had to be the least detailed self-portrait ever. I put my guard up quick and once again let no one in.

A student read her self-portrait, and she started to cry . I looked at her and then looked at my sheet, realizing mine wasn't nearly as serious as hers. She put her heart into her self-portrait as she described a very serious childhood trauma. This forced me to scribble a few things about my myself that weren't too serious, but it allowed you to understand the point of my self-portrait. By the time she finished I started to tear up. The tears would continue, as every student would continually tell very serious stories. Finally, it was my turn to go.

Through the tears I had after hearing everyone's story, I started reading my notes which were no longer notes; it was just unreadable chicken scratch. I just spoke from the heart. "My self-portrait, although not as serious as some of your stories, happened before eighth grade when my mom discovered my spine was curved. We then went to the doctor and I had an MRI to check if tumor cells were on my spine. They were. I had the cells removed and woke up from the surgery without an ability to walk. Through physical therapy, I regained my ability to walk. My senior year of high school, tumor cells appeared in my brain, and I eventually wound up on a life-support machine."

Once I was done, I read my sheet back and the only thing I had changed was the jokes, that being there were none. I don't know, maybe it was finally seeing other people confess to their traumas, but I sort of imagine it's the feeling you get at an AA meeting. I imagine the positive aspect of those meetings is hearing other people talk about the same tough struggles you're going through without being judged. Although I was nowhere near being great at talking about my life in an open forum, that class was a start.

For our final class, we performed a group theater presentation. It was me and two other students performing a three-minute scene together. Now have I mentioned that I have a learning disability, and my short-term memory is very limited? To remember a three-minute scene with other students would be a challenge.

We got our scene, and it required a lot of walking around and a lot of speaking as well. With that requirement in mind, we had to work on Sunday night for us to finally get the scene down. As we continually ran through the scene, I could see my partners get visibly frustrated every time I blew a line or I didn't walk to the proper position. Arms would be thrown up in the air and an immediate "Let's go again" would be said. They weren't acting. I could get their frustration; if they were in my major and they were failing at a group assignment we were doing it would annoy me. We trained outside of Lyman, as the building was locked. As the sun went down we chose to finally give up once it was completely dark. With the light from the sun officially down, it was time to pull away the curtain and let the show begin.

In the upset of the century, I performed my scene pretty close to perfectly. There may have been a few missteps here and there in terms of walking. I'll blame my spinal cord surgery for that. But I nailed all of my lines with precision that day. Take that, Daniel Day-Lewis! I'll be waiting for my Oscar in the mail.

My final notable achievement at Southern was a hiking class I took as an elective my senior year. This course had the same exact feel as the theater course. You take it get, an A and move on with your life. It's simple stuff. How do you fail at hiking? What if I told you, that he couldn't figure out how to hike up this mountain? (30 for 30)

For our first class, we went to a park and were given a compass. We were told to walk around the park and get used to how the compass works. Now for all my life I've been an indoors man, not an outdoors man.

I searched the park with my compass as if I was the world's greatest navigator and thought it was silly. It was 2012 at that point; the need to use a compass seemed like child's play. Give me a smart phone app and let me be. It took me about a half-hour to understand, but it came when I started to realize the greatness of being away from your phone. It was as true then as it is now: remember to take time away from your smart phone. You'll see there's a lot more to life than the latest phone.

For the next class, it was time to go hiking. Surprisingly, I didn't wake up nervous about it. Looking back on it now, it was pretty insane for me to take a hiking course. There were some days at school where I had trouble walking up the stairs. Now I'm supposed to walk in nature with rocks and all, from point A to point B back to point A.

For the first quarter-mile, I did pretty well keeping up with the group and no issues arose. Then I started to fall behind the other students. The students and the teacher didn't really have that negative of a reaction to me being far behind. I left you far behind. (Eastbound and Down) My roommate who was also a Make-A-Wish child, Jim Zarfis, was with me, too. We kept trying our best to catch up … and then it happened.

My left foot gave out, and Down goes Metz down goes Metz. I wasn't out for the count as I immediately got up, acting as if nothing happened. My professor heard the fall and ran back to make sure I was all right. I said, "I'm fine. Let's just keep going." I could've been more dramatic and said, "You're going to have to airlift me out of this park if you believe I'll stop walking." That would've been a pretty cool quote, right? Right? (Family Guy) I'll continue writing in hopes you acknowledged the coolness. I continued and made it to the end of the hike. Finishing that hike was the greatest athletic feat I had ever accomplished, other than playing basketball and baseball before November 19th, 2004. And although this wasn't considered a direct competition with someone, it was an athletic feat in my eyes. I was competing against my disabled body. I was glad to accomplish an athletic feat once again.

For the next class, we went hiking again. This time after my struggles with my 'trip heard around the world,' my professor was kind enough to bring walking sticks with him. He looked at me and offered the sticks, but for a second I thought about having too much pride and declining. I did learn to walk again while in rehab. I came back from a brain tumor. I don't need anyone's help. Before I declined, I thought about how important his actions were in bringing those walking sticks. People with disabilities are put behind their healthy counterparts. Whether it is a need for a wheelchair or the need for assistance when walking. Our challenge of going the same distance as someone who is fully healthy will always be tougher. But in the end we just want the equal opportunity to be just like them. Those walking sticks were giving me that opportunity. I smiled and took the walking sticks.

I walked through the hiking trail with my walking sticks giving me the support I needed to make it from start to finish. It was the support of those sticks that got me to the end. I completed the hike and the remaining three classes with pride.

With one more semester left, I was close to finishing my entire college career with no further health issues. Proving I could've gone to any other school without worrying about health. Was I making another mistake with my schooling by not going to a different school?

Science class became an issue for me at Southern. I completed one science course my sophomore year with no problems. The class didn't involve any labs, and everything came easy to me. I needed to complete one more science course to graduate. I picked a course with a lab, and I struggled. I don't know, maybe I'm more of a learner compared to a doer. Could that be a thing? I liked to think that could be as I put in for a 'drop' of that course. I overthought dropping that course for a couple of days. In my eyes, if you drop a course that means you're admitting defeat. I wanted to go to college and say I saw every course to the end. Believe it or not I had perfect attendance in college. Yes, that is the most uncool thing you've ever read. I guess I lost the coolness I earned earlier. Dropping a class is the greatest way of striking down a perfect attendance record. I had to though; the class was too tough for me. Every lab we went to, every student would pick up on things, while I struggled. I looked at the graded assignments and did the math in my head, and I had a D. At this point, I made the drop and left the course.

I now needed to find a new science class. I looked through the catalogue and found a physics class with no lab. By complete randomness I ended up taking the course with a great friend of mine named Hillary. She knew of my disability, so she would be helpful. When you have a disability, it's always great to have someone in your corner. Our physics course was a night class we took Wednesdays. We would walk from North Campus to Engelman Hall together. The walk was about 0.5 miles. Some nights it would be a struggle, other nights it was just a normal walk. After one class, I wasn't extremely tired and showed no symptoms of anything as I left the lecture hall. It felt like a normal day. Hillary and I both walked and talked like friends do, and all of the sudden, my left leg gave out and straight to the ground I went. It was very similar to my hiking accident. Hillary stopped walking and asked, "Are you ok?" I did my best to ignore her, as I love to remain guarded and not express my issues. I stood up on my own and kept walking with no reply. We took about ten more steps and I fell again. She looked at me and yelled, "Are you okay?!" Hearing her voice raised, I had to reply, "Yes." I kept walking. Ten more steps and I fell for a third time. This time I attempted to get up and she stood right in front of me. "Stop. Call your parents and have them bring you to the hospital." I wanted to dismiss her and say not to worry about it. The look in her eyes said she wasn't messing around. I gave in and my called my dad who brought me to Yale-New Haven Hospital. I ended up getting a shunt adjustment that day. Remember, that's what friends are for.

I ended up graduating from Southern Connecticut State University with a degree in communications and really no direction in my life. I worked with my dad part-time doing busy work around his office. That was good as it got me out of the house, but it wasn't truly me.

16

My name is Cory Metz, former make a wish child in 2009 greatest experience of my life. I really want to give back to this organization by volunteering I sent in an application about two weeks ago just want to double check if you got it or not. If you could e-mail me back that would be great thank you.

That's the e-mail that started it all (with a great amount of grammar mistakes). We will dive further into that issue later. As a writer I wish I had a better story for why I came back into the Foundation. Actually, I wish I had a story for you. I honestly can't remember how it came about. My parents never told me, hey, why don't you work with Make-A-Wish. From what I gathered from my e-mails, it just seems like I went on the Make-A-Wish Connecticut website one day and found a link saying to send your e-mail if you're willing to help. I sent my e-mail.

It was a weeknight after a day of part-time work with my dad. I drove through the dark night sky keeping my eyes wide open to the best of my ability. When you have a brain tumor you experience more fatigue—at least for me if my body doesn't get eight hours of sleep the night before. It has a quicker chance of going into shutdown mode. Shutdown mode meaning I would just be tired. The night before I was working on about seven hours of sleep. This meant I should've just stayed home and rested. On the days I get seven hours of sleep, lying on the couch is about the greatest thing I can accomplish after working for eight hours. Making it to this training will be tough, but I have to try.

I went to the Make-A-Wish office and it looked like the entire office building was closed. All of the lights were turned off. The entrance door was locked with no signs of humans ever working in this building. Was this a sign? Maybe this Make-A-Wish thing wasn't for me. I called Cheryl Beiling, as she was the volunteer coordinator who I talked with about coming back into the foundation. There was no answer. I stood by the door and frantically opened pulled at the locked door, as if something would change.

What was the point? I was defeated and it was time to pack my bags up and never volunteer for Make-A-Wish. The book ends here. I hope you enjoyed the book. The rest of this book is just filler as my publisher wanted a set number of pages. You'll see it's just a mess of words with zero context if you keep turning pages. Go ahead, I dare you. Did you look?

As I was about to walk away, a woman came from the parking lot and attempted to open the door too. She also called Cheryl and got no answer. The woman looked at me and asked, "What do we do?" I shrugged and started walking toward my car. She started to walk up a tiny hill and noticed there were lights on up there. That's where we needed to go. She yelled, "The workshop is this way." I followed with delight as my Make-A-Wish experience wasn't over, yet. As with most of the things in this book it had an interesting start. Please read the rest of this book I was joking about the fact it's all filler. I think the heart of the story is actually beyond this page. Consider this part of the book our designated intermission. Feel free to stretch your legs.

I snuck into the back for the workshop, as I was late. Something I hated to do.

A PowerPoint presentation was put on by a person who I assumed was Cheryl, and the presentation ended with her thanking everyone for coming. I snuck out not saying goodbye or even saying hello, as Cheryl didn't even know me. Of course, I was Cory Metz, wish kid from 2009, and I imagine there's some record of me in the office. But she didn't know the actual person. Cathie and Georgianna, my wish grantors knew who Cory was. People in the office didn't truly know me. I hope with the work I will put into the foundation, they will know me then.

17

Disclaimer: I asked all of the wish families being talked about in this story if I could write about my experience with their children. I told them I would change their names and I'm just writing about my experience in helping grant their wishes. Every family has allowed me to write about my experience in granting a wish to their children.

I contacted Cheryl, and she gave me my first wish to help fulfill through e-mail. Before I go in-depth as to what happened on my first wish-granting experience, let me explain what a wish grantor does exactly. As a wish grantor you get e-mails every Thursday stating that new kids who've been put through the wish referral process and are eligible for a wish. Once you read the e-mail you put your name down for a specific wish. Cheryl picks out two people who are signed up for a child's wish and they become that child's wish grantors. Once that process is complete the two wish grantors get in contact through e-mail and a phone call and pick out a wide range of dates and times to visit with the child. Once they agree on that range one of them calls the wish family. The person who calls the family asks the time and date their family would be available for a meeting and what the interests of the children in the family are. Once those things are established you e-mail the office and let them know the date you're going.

Cheryl e-mailed my partner, Julia, telling her it was my first wish and asking if she could take the lead. Julia e-mailed back and gladly accepted. She e-mailed me telling me she would call to schedule a date with the family and asked if I had preferred time. I replied, any time after five on weekdays and anytime on the weekend works. Julia sent back one final e-mail, stating she would call tonight, and we were off.

The day of the wish came and we met Dan. Dan was six years old and he was a very quiet kid. He looked at the both of us with strange curiosity and went back to his couch. Which I could understand at six years old. I would be afraid to talk with complete strangers walking into my house at that age. Come to think of it, I had that same feeling at eighteen with Georgianna and Cathie came to my house.

I took a seat at the other end of the couch opposite Dan while Julia found a chair to sit in, and she talked about the foundation. She stated how we were here to grant Dan's wish. If Dan could ask for any wish in the world we at the foundation will try our best to grant it. Both of Dan's parents looked at us in amazement while Dan was playing with toy cars Julia brought for him. Dan walked over to me and handed me one of his cars and then pushed his car straight toward mine. Here's the thing … I didn't have cousins or a little brother growing up. I've never had the experience of playing with cars with a child. I played video games against my older brother as a child; I didn't play with cars. Before Dan's car came crashing into mine; I had to think about what to do here. Do I crash my toy car into his, or do I let his toy car come to me? What's proper protocol? I decided to hold back, and Dan knocked my car out of my hand and I pretended it exploded. Dan laughed and continued to grab other cars and pretend to drive them on his couch. He would hand trucks to me and look at me wanting me to follow him with cars. I was sure to follow, but not too close. That's a lesson I learned in driving school; if you follow too closely, you could cause an accident. Let that be an important lesson in this book, kids.

Dan continued to steer his cars, while Julia was able to establish Dan's wish with his parents. They agreed that going to Walt Disney World would be the best idea for Dan. The paperwork was written up and the visit came to an end. Dan would go to Disney and enjoy his trip.

18

My vision for volunteering with the Make-A-Wish Foundation was that I always make friends with a child who's into sports. The type of child who enjoys sports, and through my experiences in life, I can get him to his true wish. Through some very rewarding work, Jerry became that child.

After completing my first wish with a six year old who went to Disney, I emailed the foundation and asked to grant another wish. The foundation sent me a reply saying my next wish is with a ten year old named Jerry, and that your wish partner is Cathie. Cathie, Cathie, Cathie. That name did sound familiar to me. Is it Cathie Bates? Do you remember when she was a guest star on The Office? I checked the spelling on the email and it was spelled differently. I read the last name … Allen.

Cathie Allen was my wish grantor in 2009. I stared at that email and thought, wow what a full circle type of moment. I'll be seeing Cathie again, but this time we will be working together and granting a child's wish. Instead of sitting across from her at the table, I'll be sitting to the right of her as we work together to get a child's wish. This will be truly a magical experience.

Cathie told me she set up the initial wish visit to meet Jerry, but there was one thing— Cathie wanted to meet before we visited Jerry. I looked at Google Maps and spotted a Panera Bread that was close to Jerry's address. Panera Bread—when you're here, you're family. Is that Panera Bread? I'll have my research team figure that out.

Driving to Panera to meet Cathie, I reflected on what she did for me five years ago. It was Cathie who took time out of her day to come help grant my wish. It was Cathie who helped steer me to my one true wish. It was now my job to do exactly what Cathie did for me. No pressure.

I arrived early and took a deep breath in and out. While walking toward the entrance of Panera, my body started to shake, as it tends to do when I'm nervous. With the shakes came the 'what if' game, a game I always play when I'm nervous. What if Cathie forgets who I am? What if Jerry and his family dislike me? What if this all worked out? I hoped that third question was true.

I found a table and waited for Cathie to enter. After about five minutes, I spotted a woman looking around for someone. I had to assume that was Cathie, as she looked vaguely familiar.

Cathie came over, and I got out of the booth to give her a hug. We hugged and she said, "Could you believe this Cory, we're here five years later working together, I mean, how cool is this?" I replied, "Yeah, it's very cool." What a cool response. I'm back baby. (Seinfeld)

We both sat down together, and Cathie pulled out Jerry's paperwork. Cathie began to describe her wish process, as she knew I was new at this. "With Jerry's age, what I like to do is put him and his parents in the kitchen and we can work his wish ideas out. If he's shy, his parents can help. But, if his parents become too much and it's really becoming the parents wish and not the child's wish, we will ask them to leave. How does that sound?"

"Yeah, I remember you told me and my parents to go toward the kitchen five years ago." "Haha, that's right."

Cathie made sure to double check she had all the proper paperwork, and we left for Jerry's house. His house was only a couple of minutes away, and my nerves came right back as we exited Panera and I opened my car door. The question of what if Jerry's family dislikes me still came to mind.

I followed Cathie to Jerry's, and within two minutes we were there. We both exited our cars and Cathie asked, "Are you ready?" I nodded that I was ready as I'll ever be, and Jerry's wish had officially begun.

Cathie rang the doorbell and Jerry's mom came to the door. She looked at both of us and waved through the glass door. She opened the door and couldn't have been happier to meet us. She looked at Cathie and told her, "It's great to finally meet you in person after our phone calls." Cathie replied, "Same to you."

Cathie turned to me and said, "This is Cory. He's my other wish grantor, and he'll be helping throughout this wish process too." Jerry's mom shook my hand and said, "It's great to meet you too, Cory." Cathie took a seat at the kitchen table and called Jerry and his father over.

Cathie led the discussion by asking Jerry, "Do you know what the Make-A-Wish Foundation is?

That was the question I was asked five years ago. I saw wishes being granted on ESPN's SportsCenter; outside of that, I had no idea. Jerry looked at us and smiled. He knew a little, but not that much.

Cathie told Jerry it was our job to get him to his one true wish. "If there's anything in the world you want, tell us and we will try to make it come true." Jerry started to smile even more knowing he could ask for anything. Jerry had one wish idea that stuck out.

"I wish to meet Jennifer Lawrence."

Once Jerry suggested Jennifer Lawrence, all four of us looked at each other thinking that what he just said was a joke. And with me having impeccable comedic timing, I told Jerry I would like to meet Jennifer Lawrence too. That did get some laughs. Jerry's mom asked, "Are you sure you want to meet Jennifer Lawrence?" Jerry's dad said, "I had no idea you even knew who Jennifer Lawrence was."

Jerry laughed, but kept a straight face after his laughter, indicating that his one true wish was really to meet Jennifer Lawrence.

Cathie looked at him and asked, "Is this your true wish?" Jerry replied, "Yes, I want to meet Jennifer Lawrence." Cathie smiled as she saw through his body language that this is what he wants. "Okay we'll send off an e-mail to the foundation, and we'll keep in touch with your parents."

Cathie and I shook hands with Jerry's parents and told them they'll be receiving an e-mail or a phone call shortly. Before we both left to go home, Cathie stopped me and said, "That was interesting." I said, "Yeah, who would've guessed Jennifer Lawrence."

Cathie sent an e-mail to the foundation stating that Jerry wants meet Jennifer Lawerence, Almost immediately the foundation e-mailed Cathie back telling her they have a date to meet Jennifer Lawrence. The foundation then asked if they should add Jerry to the list of wish kids around the world who want to meet Jennifer Lawerence? Then all of the sudden Cathie replied to the foundation stating to not put Jerry on the list. I read the start of that e-mail and thought, did something happen to Jerry? Please, don't tell me something happened to Jerry. He seemed fine two weeks ago. It pains me to come to this realization, but this is a foundation meant for sick children. At any moment something bad could happen to these children. Please don't tell me something happened to Jerry. I continued to read the e-mail, and Jerry's mom said that she talked to her son and they both came to their realization together that meeting Jennifer Lawrence wasn't his true wish.

With that Cathie called me a couple of days later wanting to talk about Jerry's wish process. She called me explaining her conversation with Jerry's mom.

"So, I talked with Jerry's mom and she told me Jerry is still very undecided about his wish." You being a former wish kid, would you be comfortable with talking to Jerry about your wish process?" Would I be comfortable with talking about my wish process? I'm not comfortable with talking to people behind the deli counter. I had some trepidation.

For Jerry though, I had to do it. I was the only person he knew who could truly steer him in the correct direction. I had to send Jerry off to his one true wish. His bags are packed. Just send him home. (Happy Gilmore)

Now I had to figure out the best way to present my wish process to Jerry. I walked around my room and thought out loud. Do I write a paper and hand it to Jerry? No, that would be too long. Then my eyes went straight to my dresser and there it was. It was my picture standing next to David Wright. That one picture says it all. It's coming to the wish idea that will give you the exact same smile I had standing next to my hero, David Wright. I grabbed the picture and brought it with me as part of a visual presentation for Jerry. I've always been a big fan of visuals; I feel like they put less pressure on the speaker as the listener can sometimes look at either you or the visual when you are presenting.

Cathie decided to buy pizza to help ease the stress for Jerry, as she imagined this process had become somewhat burdensome. We meet at Giove's Pizza Kitchen, and I told her about my idea and she thought it was brilliant. Cathie grabbed the pizza and drove off to Jerry's once again.

Cathie placed the pizzas on the table and all five of us had one slice. Everyone seemed to be looking at my photo that I brought from home me with my sports hero David Wright, which meant it was time for me to speak. Cathie introduced the idea to Jerry by saying, "Cory has something to share with you." I looked at Jerry as he sat directly across from me. Luckily I didn't see Billy Bob Thornton in Jerry's eyes, so I was loud and ready to talk with Jerry.

"So for me it was fairly simple. The thing I've enjoyed my entire life is watching sports. While watching sports I've always been more fascinated with the box scores compared to the actual games. I've always been interested in the league leaders of each sport. Realizing that I had to think about All-Star games. After that I thought about the three major sports I enjoyed the most: NBA, NFL, and MLB. I picked the MLB All-Star weekend because I felt like that was the largest event. The Home Run Derby and the actual All-Star Game will bring the most happiness. All the secret stuff in between grew the wish to an unbelievable level. Here's my photo with David Wright, my favorite athlete." Jerry looked at the photo closely and said, "That's cool."

Cathie brought some posterboard and markers with her and said, "Whatever idea you have about your wish, write it down on this posterboard. We'll come back once you have enough ideas you're comfortable with." Jerry loved that idea and you could tell by his newly formed smile that he had some ideas rolling around in his mind.

Cathie and I said goodbye once again to Jerry's family. Cathie stopped me before I could leave and said, "Good job Cory, and I think we'll get to the heart of his one true wish now."

Although Cathie's reassurance was completely unnecessary, as I knew I had helped Jerry a little it was nice to hear that coming from my former wish grantor. Especially knowing what she did for me in 2009.

A couple of months later Cathie sent me an e-mail telling me Jerry has his wish idea in mind, and he wants to tell us about. I read her e-mail and thought, What could it possibly be?

Cathie knocked on Jerry's door for what we believed to be the last time. Jerry's mom came to open the door for us once more. Jerry was sitting at the kitchen table once again, this time smiling while his poster board sat on the table. Cathie and I both sat at the kitchen table and Cathie asked, "What do you have for us?" Jerry looked at us and said, "I want to meet Curtis Granderson of the New York Mets."

I was stunned to say the least. He wanted to do a baseball wish that was fairly similar to my wish. I couldn't have been happier. Jerry talked about a limo ride, throwing out the first pitch; every idea a boy could think of, he thought of it. That's what the wish process is about.

Cathie e-mailed the foundation to let them know Jerry had his wish idea in mind. It would be a few months before Jerry's wish would come true because he had made his decision in August.

In the meantime we had to work on Jerry's wish delivery party. Jerry had his delivery party at InSports in Trumbull. They were nice enough to allow Jerry and his friends to use of the facility one weekend morning. It's beautiful to see when companies take time out of their days to help wish kids. Nothing puts a brighter smile on my face as a volunteer with the organization.

Before the trip to InSports, Cathie called me and asked, "Would you mind making a speech with me?" I thought about it, and I did do pretty well last time I gave my speech to Jerry about the wish process. I knew I could do it and agreed.

The day came as I pulled into the parking lot early. Cathie came five minutes later with her husband as they helped set up food and cleaned up the entrance for Jerry as she put a welcome sign up and life-size cut out of him next to the welcome sign.

I walked over to the wiffle ball field and helped set up the bases and pitcher's mound. Everything was all set, and as soon as we were done kids and families came pouring in. It was great to see so many kids and families that cared for Jerry in his time of need. As everyone was playing, I walked over to the bench and pulled my speech out of my pocket. I studied that sheet as if it was a study guide for a final exam. I wanted to cross parts out, but I didn't have a pen. Cathie came over to me and asked, "Is that your speech?" I looked at her and replied, "It is."

"Do you mind if I read it?" I handed it over. She read it and said, "You'll be fine Cory, there's no need to worry." That was the reassurance I needed.

Cathie looked at her watch and asked me if I was ready. I told her I was. She said, "Great, now we just need to find Jerry." I pointed toward Jerry, and Cathie told him to walk with us. Jerry, Cathie, and I climbed the stairs and Cathie said, "Thank you everyone for coming today. You've all shown you have a deep appreciation for Jerry by being here today and we thank you for showing that appreciation. Next to me I have Cory Metz; he's a former wish kid and he would like to say a few words.

"First off I want to thank InSports, Big Y, and everyone here for coming today to celebrate Jerry's wish party. Let me start off by saying I am former wish child. Back in 2009, I received my wish from the Make-A-Wish foundation. My wish was to go to the 2009 MLB All-Star weekend. It was without question the greatest weekend of my life. What Make-A-Wish gave me was a weekend to forget about my health problems and just be a happy kid once again. That's what the Make-A-Wish foundation does; it provides an escape for every child they provide wishes for. My request is for you to tell your friends, because none of this would be possible without donations and volunteers. When you look at a kid like Jerry and see the smile on his face after you tell him he's going to meet Curtis Granderson of the New York Mets, there isn't a greater feeling on earth. Finally, Let's Go Mets!"

I can't remember if anyone clapped when my speech was over or if anyone really listened. I could care less about the audience. I just wanted to know if the person standing next to me took that speech in. If he did, my hope is I'll be seeing him grant wishes in the future.

I walked down the stairs and went to grab some food now that the pressure of my speech was done. After I grabbed a few chips, I turned around and Jerry was standing behind me. I looked at him and wanted to say, "Jerry what are you doing? Go enjoy your party." Jerry looked at me and handed me a box. I held the box and said, "This is completely unnecessary." I opened the box, and it was a keychain that said the word "wish" on it. I started to think about that one word that will bond the two of us for the rest of our lives as wish kids. I thanked Jerry and told him I'll be sure to always hold onto this. The keychain is on my dresser, and every morning I look at it and remember our wish experience together.

[]

19

During this time, I was working part-time at my dad's office, IUOE Local 478. They would throw busy work around the office at me, and I would come in on a part-time basis. It was anything but exciting, but it was a paycheck and something to do. I appreciated that, as my job prospects after college were non-existent. I still wasn't doing what I wanted in terms of employment.

I was lost, and then a substitute teacher who worked with my mom suggested applying to the Sports Business Management program at Manhattanville College. I ended up getting in, and I was back to school once again.

My time at Manhattanville went pretty well. I finished with a 3.4 GPA and at least in the beginning, I was fascinated by every class. Knowing how the sports world worked from a business perspective was something I never thought about as a kid. I watched ESPN, but you never think about what ESPN does as a business. How do they operate day-to-day? With all of their properties, how does the sports business world work? I started to learn daily.

I was commuting to Manhattanville, and it wasn't as fun as one would imagine. In my opinion commuting to college stinks. For me, I enjoy life being close and simple. Put in on the poll, do most introverts hate commuting? (The Dan Le Batard Show) Just keep it simple and easy. When you make things tough and hard that's when life becomes tough for me. That day came for me on one commute to school.

Traffic accidents are a thing that happens; that's why they're called accidents. My car accident came when I was going a little over the speed limit. I was traveling south on the Merritt Parkway a few exits away from where I had my minor seizure a few years earlier. As I coasted in the left lane of the Merritt Parkway, which is a lane meant for cars to pass in, a car speed past me in the right lane. It was like a cartoon as the car drove past me. Unaware I wasn't in a racing game, I did my best to catch this passer. I ended up tailing him for a bit, but eventually the car came out of my view as the car bobbed and weaved through cars driving at normal speeds. At this point I realized I wasn't playing a game of Grand Theft Auto and slowed down a little bit. As I slowed down, I wished everything in front of me continued to go slower.

I was back in the left lane and then all of the sudden, bang! I ended up hitting the car in front of me. It wasn't the best moment of my life as I pulled over to the side. I got out of car and looked forward to see that the car that sped past me had caused a chain reaction. Thanks to that speeding car that passed me earlier.

After I had a conversation with the driver, who pointed out it was the person who drove like a psycho in front of her that caused the accident, I called my mom, as she's always been the person I reach out to if I'm in trouble.

I told her about the accident. I told it in the sad voice you have when you have to tell your mom you did something wrong. I confessed, "Hi, I was driving too fast and hit a car on the Merritt Parkway." She said, "Are you okay?" "I just got into the accident, and I saw the car has minimal damage." This time I was yelled at: "Are you okay?" "Yeah I am fine. It was a minor accident." "Okay, I don't care about the car just tell me if you're alright."

"Sorry." "It's okay and if you don't want to go to class, don't go to class." I thought about that statement, and as I waited for the police to come and investigate the accident, I wondered if I should miss class?

The police car pulled in behind my car. The cop exited his car to talk about the accident. I told him how the accident in front of us set off a chain reaction and caused me to hit the car. He nodded and asked for my license and registration. After he had a conversation with the driver in the vehicle in front of me he stated, "Although the car in front did set off a reaction, you were still following too close. I'll have to give you a ticket." I took the ticket with a little bit of an upset smirk as no one wants to get a ticket. The cop stopped traffic and allowed me to pull back onto the highway, and I had to think about going to school. Should I just exit the highway and go back home or continue to school and go to class? At this point I would just be a few minutes late for class. It just became a question of if this accident was too traumatic for me to continue my drive. I decided to continue on the Merritt Parkway, and I walked into the classroom at the same time as my professor. The lesson is to keep on keeping on. That was my best attempt at a Matthew McConaughey type of a quote for this book. Did I nail it?

After the accident my parents suggested I live at a dorm on Manhattanville's campus. I learned one lesson from living on campus as a graduate student, and that is graduate students on campus aren't the coolest kids on campus. It's the undergraduate students who have the clubs and everything designed for them. Because of that my life on campus for a second time was incredibly boring. In a way it was similar to my time at Southern Connecticut State University. I'm sure there were certain things that were designed for graduate students in terms of interaction with other graduate students; I choose to not seek them out. Was that my disability stopping me from attempting to interact with others? Probably. Whatever it was, I was living a pretty lonely life in college. I would go get my meals alone, study, and then sleep. Again, I did end up with a 3.4 GPA by the time I graduated, so I did do something right.

That summer my dad helped me get an internship with the Nutmeg State Games. I took that internship as I was in a bind, since I was getting closer to graduation and I hadn't secured an internship yet. I sent my resume to some places but didn't get a response. I went to my dad and told him I couldn't find any internships. My dad (being the most caring guy I know) told me about the Nutmeg State Games and got me a meeting with Patrick Fisher the manager of the Games.

We had a conversation for about a minute, and I realized this internship worked for me. I shook hands with Patrick and was told the start date.

I looked at the date, and it was the same day I bought tickets for the Foo Fighters at Citi Field. Can you name a better band that fights Foo? I can't think of one. In my eyes, Dave Grohl was a hero of mine. That should be a song. What makes Dave Grohl so heroic to me is the fact he was in greatest band ever in my mind, Nirvana. After the band had to dissolve because of Kurt Cobain's passing, Dave Grohl grieved but knew he still loved music and wanted to continue with his career. He formed a new life with a new band and created one of the greatest rock bands ever. I liked to think I was doing the same thing with my work at Make-A-Wish. Yes, me being a wish kid is tough, and I've had a tough life. But I can't sit in my grief and just continually feel bad for myself. I have to do something more with my life. Although my wish happened and it was over with, I was forming new wishes with every single new wish I volunteered for.

I decided to give my ticket to my brother, and he ended up enjoying the show while I spent the day learning about the Nutmeg State Games. I wasn't that upset about it as I had been learning through the Foundation that it's better to give than to receive. Patrick Fisher told us about the Nutmeg State Games. He stated how this was an amateur competition for people in Connecticut. It's another way for athletes to show off their skills. It was a nice idea to learn about, and I looked forward to working with the Games.

We got to stay in the dorms at Central Connecticut State University. That day a new season of BoJack Horseman came out the first night in the dorms. This was my reason to stay in my dorm that night and not interact with anyone. Maybe this was my disability talking once again by not leaving my dorm, or I just loved BoJack Horseman. I like to think it was both. As I overheard interns in the program interacting with each other. All I heard was Bojack Horseman just horsing around.

My internship responsibility was going to events around New Britain and setting up for the competition that day. Although it was slow and boring to set up events for others, it was great to see the work I put in every morning as athletes stepped onto the baseball field, soccer field, and basketball courts I worked on. It was the sense of doing something in the morning for others and then seeing them enjoy what you've done for them in the afternoon. It was very similar to what Cathie and I did for Jerry.

After I completed watching the entire season of Bojack Horseman the most important thing in my life I walked out to common room where everyone was hanging out. I ended up bringing an N64 to the Nutmeg State Games as video games had always been a connection in my life. There was a television in the common room at Central Connecticut. I placed my N64 in the middle of the room after connecting it to the television and we all started to play. The lesson is Mario Kart 64 can be the great connector this world needs.

The internship ended, and in all honesty I wasn't that happy about the work I just put in. As far as working in sports as a career, I was indifferent to it after completing my internship. Students complete internships and then say that this is what I want to do with my life. If my feelings were an emoji it would be the mouth that's just a line. I wrote this line before the movie The Emoji Movie came out in hopes that it would be so successful that making an emoji reference would be a good idea. I hope I made the right choice.

I went back to Manhattanville to complete my degree because I don't believe in quitting, even though I wasn't too confident in a degree in sports business management working for me. I actually gave a presentation about how bad concussions are for players, and if you truly cared for football players lives, you would turn the game into two-hand touch. An idea my professor questioned and stated, "I don't think that's the only solution." It wasn't the most pro-sports business topic to bring up. Maybe I was wrong at the time, and I was looking at players' health strictly through the lens of someone who actually lost everything and had to rebuild his brain in a hospital. I wouldn't want that to happen to any of my favorite NFL players. Concussions have been down from the time I made that presentation. And I hope the NFL will continue to do their best, because as someone who did experience a traumatic brain injury and still dealing with the ramifications, I believe no one should ever go through that.

The second thing I brought up was stating how owners should pay for their own stadiums. I made sure to say that no taxpayer money should ever fund a stadium. Again, this is not the most pro-sports business idea. I stayed in the program because I don't believe in quitting anything and I grabbed my degree with some hesitation at the graduation ceremony.

I went back to my dad's job and continued to work part-time while sending out my resume to sports companies around Connecticut. I was too afraid to look outside of Connecticut as leaving the Yale-New Haven Hospital area would've been too much for me. The doctors knew my story, and the trust was there with Yale. To look at jobs outside of Connecticut wasn't an option for me. Because of that, nothing came as I sent my resume to different companies. That put me in a slight depression, as my time in the program meant nothing. Where is my life going?

20

I did the next logical thing when I couldn't find full-time employment; I told Make-A-Wish Connecticut that I wanted to come back into the program as a wish grantor. I had left because I was living in Purchase, New York, and commuting back and forth for Make-A-Wish would be impossible.

Another day, and another new wish was on the horizon. My hope was this new wish would be just like Jerry's wish. If the wish child was indecisive about the wish he wanted, I would speak up and tell him about my wish process. We work together through our conversation and we get to his one true wish. It sounds simple enough in theory. But as you'll learn in this book, no wish in the Make-A-Wish Foundation is ever the same.

I just graduated from grad school with a degree in sports business management, and I was lost. After my graduation, I sent a few applications to a few sports companies, but unfortunately nothing came of it. There were some nerves as I wondered what I would do with my life. There wasn't a feeling of bitterness though; I believe everything in this life happens for a reason. My mom always preached that statement to me. Even when my mom saw her son in the ICU on life support, a very small part of her still held that belief. I feel as long as you continually do the right thing and help others in life, good things will come your way. The way I did the right thing and helped others was by being a wish grantor at the Make-A-Wish Foundation.

My next wish was with a child named George. Being out of the Foundation for almost two years while in school did cause some anxiety. Can I still re-create the Make-A-Wish magic I created a year-and-a-half ago? George was fifteen. His being a teenager was somewhat comforting. Getting that one-on-one experience of communication with the wish child is exactly what I'm comfortable with.

I received a phone call from my other wish partner Julie. Julie had been working in the Foundation for a few years and understood what it took to create the power of a wish. That also calmed my nerves, as having an experienced wish grantor with me certainly helped, as this was only my third wish.

During our phone call Julie asked, "How long have you been in the Foundation?" I replied, "In and out for four years." I probably could've expanded on that, but I don't do that.

Julie asked, "Do you want to me to be the lead wish grantor then?" I replied, "Yes, if you could." She replied, "Of course."

The next step was meeting George. George lived 40 minutes away from my job. Julie was 20 minutes away the opposite way. Through e-mail I asked Julie if we could carpool together as my commute was a little further considering it was a weekday. Julie was kind enough to say that we could. It also gave us time to discuss a strategy in terms of communication with the wish child.

Julie and I agreed to meet in a commuter parking lot halfway between the both of us. I arrived early, as I tend to always do, and sat in the parking lot waiting for Julie. I thought about my approaches for helping George with his wish. Within seconds I realized there wasn't anything to strategize with George. George was the Make-A-Wish child I always envisioned working with. Although I was eighteen the day I discussed my wish with my two wish grantors, I was still a teenager. I could still relate to how George was feeling with his wish experience.

After my epiphany, I spotted a car pulling into the commuter parking lot. Julie described her car and color in an earlier text. I checked the text and knew that was Julie. I opened my car door and walked over to Julie's car. Once I opened her passenger door, I was officially back in the Make-A-Wish Foundation.

Julie pulled out of the commuter lot and we started to discuss George's wish as she drove to his house. "With George's age I like to let him open up from the start. With his age I'm sure he'll be ready to open up to us. If he needs guidance we will be there to guide him if need be. If George is not ready we will be willing to wait." I never really thought about the way to approach a wish. What Julie was saying may have been the most basic statement you'll ever hear in your life. But it rang incredibly true. As wish grantors, our job is to go into the child's house and let them speak. It's not our job to steer them in any direction. Just let the wish child speak.

Julie pulled up to the street where George's apartment was. We both exited the car at the same time and walked toward the door. Julie called George's mother to alert her that we were downstairs. We waited for a minute and the door opened with George's mother saying hello to the both of us. She smiled and said, "Please come follow me to the elevator." We followed as she thanked us for coming and told us her son will be so happy. All three of us exited the elevator together and walked toward George's apartment.

We entered the apartment, and on the couch sat George. Looking at George you could clearly see a boy who was tired. He was in the hospital a week earlier for what I had assumed was some type of treatment. You could see George's battle was taking something out of him as he didn't stand up and just waved as we walked in. You could see in George's eyes he wanted to come over and greet us. His body was just saying no that day. In no way could I possibly blame him, as I had days where my body wouldn't want to move either.

Julie and I both sat near George, as we didn't want George to get up since he seemed tired. Julie led the entire speech on what the Make-A-Wish Foundation was about, and you could see George's face and demeanor change in front of our eyes. His smile started to grow as Julie finished explaining what the Make-A-Wish Foundation was trying to do for him. George looked at both of us and started to think of ideas.

He was surprisingly undecided on his wish. He told us he didn't know what he wanted. Immediately Julie jumped in and asked, "Well what is the one thing you always dreamed about in life? What about new clothes for when you go back to school?" I looked at her when she said that and thought, what does that mean? Could school lead to a child's wish? School is the last thing I ever wanted to talk about as a wish kid. I hated knowing other students were moving ahead while I was lying in a hospital bed, although it was the place I wish I was instead of the hospital bed. I preferred being told about math and science instead of being told about the tumors in my body.

After hearing that, George told us he wanted to go on a shopping spree in the mall. He told us he wanted 'new everything' to bring with him to school in late August. His wish totally made sense to me. I hate to admit this because in a way there's nothing fair about what happens to wish children. But their lives are changed forever because of their illness. One day a child is perfectly healthy and then the next day they're sick and in a hospital. There's nothing fair about what happens to them. I knew for George that getting his shopping spree would bring him back to being normal. His friends will talk to him about his new things instead of his health. That's how George's wish made sense to me, as someone who never wanted to open up about his health. Or maybe George's shopping spree held a different meaning. I didn't ask as his wish choice was his decision.

Julie and I looked at each other and she said, "That's great, we'll send this information off to the foundation." We said goodbye to George as he waved back at us.

George's mom walked us out of the apartment and thanked us for coming. She stopped us before walking toward the stairs. "Thanks for coming to help George today. These past few months have been very draining on George, and I know this experience will help him."

I didn't have a response for George's mom. I just looked at her and thought about the child we just met. He was clearly very tired and probably would've preferred to sleep that day, instead of having a conversation with strangers. But by the end of our conversation he was clearly happy and smiling. It was now my responsibility along with Julie to make his wish complete and to see that smile throughout the rest of his wish.

Now when it comes to a shopping spree wish, the wish grantors have to visit every store the wish child wants to visit and let them know a wish child will be visiting them. As a person who hated to ask for anything or ever bother anyone for anything, I hated having to do this. You have to have a certain personality to ask strangers for things. I don't have that type of personality. Thinking back to George sitting on that couch and knowing how strong he was, I had to change my personality for him.

George told us seven places he would like to visit in the mall. We also needed to talk with mall security and tell them the day George would be shopping. I told Julie I would visit GameStop, Finish Line, Foot Locker, and Track 23. I just needed to find a weekend that was open for me to go to the mall with the courage to talk with others about the Make-A-Wish Foundation.

I arrived at the mall and it wasn't as crowded as I thought it would be. Which was good for me as an introvert who's afraid of people. My motto has always been the less people around the better. I believe that same motto is found somewhere in the Gettysburg Address. Before you fact check that joke, Abe Lincoln was a known introvert. So there's some small truth. Kind of.

I walked toward GameStop first because they are a known sponsor to the Make-A-Wish Foundation. I knew walking into their store that I wouldn't be met with confusion as I talked about the foundation. There was some comfort in that.

Entering the store, a massive line stood in front of the cashier—and by that I mean eight people were standing in line. I could handle seven people standing in line, but eight, that's more than seven. I turned around and found another store on George's list.

The next store I tried was Finish Line. I remembered George talking about being a sneaker head. I found an employee and told him I had a Make-A-Wish child coming, and I was wondering if he could make sure he's here to help him. He looked at me and said, "That sounds like a real possibility; let me just double check with my manager and she'll make sure it happens." I stood and waited for someone to walk over and thought about touching all of the shoes. After I thought about it, I realized I'm here to help with George's day, not mine. Don't worry about the shoes.

The manager came out from the back and asked, "How can I help you?" I looked at her and told her the same story about helping a Make-A-Wish child. She smiled and said of course, just repeat the date and I'll write it down so I can easily be reminded. I thanked her for taking the time and told her it will mean a lot more to George.

The next store I moved to was Foot Locker. I told them about George and his wanting to come there for his wish. The person at the cash register looked at me and said, "That sounds great. I'll just need to go through corporate to see if we can do anything special for George." I looked up at her and said, "That's all I want, thank you very much."

The final store I went to before trying again at GameStop was Track 23. A store I had never heard of, but apparently they have good clothing, and whatever George wants on his mall trip George will get. I went up to the cashier and told her I worked for Make-A-Wish and I had a Make-A-Wish child coming to her store. She looked back at me and told me that they don't donate to people coming to the store. I was thrown by this comment, and she was clearly confused. I laughed it off and clarified. "I just wanted to let you know I'll have a Make-A-Wish child entering your store, and the Foundation will be paying for everything. It's not a solicitation. She laughed and asked for the date. She told me she'd be sure to have an employee come from the back room to help George when he walks in. I thanked her and walked back to GameStop.

This time the line in GameStop was non-existent. Which is just the way I like it. I walked up to the employee behind the register and told him what's going on. He got his manager, and he wanted to confirm the exact date and find out who to contact about setting something special up for the wish child. I gave him the contact information, and I thanked him for taking the time. That was it; my work was done for the day.

I e-mailed Julie telling her I knocked four stores off the list. She replied, "That's great! I'll take care of the rest and we'll be all set." We were planning the perfect day, and I couldn't wait to experience it with George.

The day of George's wish finally came, and it was an indescribable feeling. What makes a shopping spree wish different is the wish grantor is there to see the entire wish through. When you send a kid to Disney or to meet the Mets, you just get pictures back. You don't go to Orlando or Citi Field. With a shopping spree wish you get to see the wish from the beginning to the end. What an experience.

Julie and I arrived at the mall an hour before it opened as Julie had discussed with the mall manager when she visited the mall on her own. We were told by the mall manager that a mall employee would be there to let us in before the mall opened and help with setting things up. We wanted to map everything out and make sure the mall manager could help us out before our adventure began if need be. We asked her if she had a red carpet for George as he entered the mall. It turns out they did! I watched her roll the red carpet across the floor and thought back to my wish when I stood next to the red carpet at the 2009 All-Star Game. That day, I was watching future Hall-of-Fame baseball players like Mariano Rivera, Derek Jeter, Ichiro Suzuki, and Albert Pujols walk by me. They are truly the greatest baseball players of their generation. My anticipation in seeing George walk down the red carpet was greater. In my eyes, George had accomplished more in his life than any baseball player will ever accomplish. George wasn't batting against 100 mph fastballs. George wasn't closing out the seventh game of the World Series. George was facing a health crisis, and what I would describe as a greater duel compared to batting in the seventh game of the World Series. George was my Hall-of-Famer, and I couldn't wait to see him again.

George's limo ride finally pulled up to the front of the mall. He walked toward the entrance and saw Julie and I standing next to the red carpet. He started to smile and looked at both of us in embarrassment as to say, "Why would you go through this trouble?" That was a true teenager move. For you, George, it was no trouble. Julie yelled in a joking manner, "Come on and walk the red carpet, George!" George walked that carpet as if he was at the Oscar's. The only thing we were missing was hundreds of photographers. George continued to walk toward us and said thanks in his typical quiet voice. My hope was that George wasn't tired yet. George had to know his adventure was just beginning. GameStop allowed us to come into their store before they opened to allow George to look around all by himself without any other customers. That was the kind of selfless act I loved to see. Here's an employee coming in early to work to help a Make-A-Wish kid out when he didn't have to. He also brought donut munchkins for George to enjoy while he shopped. That brought a tear to my eye. George ended up buying a Nintendo Switch with a few games and accessories. By the time George was done, the mall was officially open to everyone, and George was ready to shop his entire list of stores. George went back to his limo to drop off all of his purchases from GameStop, and you could see he was even happier once he put all of gifts in the car.

Now it was time for some shoe shopping. We went to Finish Line. George found some good buys, and the staff at the stores was very helpful.

George continued to walk ahead of Julie and I with a sense of pride. I could see him thinking to himself, this is my day and everything that's happened to me in the past is now in the past. George made a left turn to Foot Locker and the employees were holding signs for George as he walked in. The Foot Locker team also gave him a gift bag, a Foot Locker shirt, and a nametag. Again it was another senseless act performed by a company.

George had his shoes and clothes all set, and now it was time for lunch at Buffalo Wild Wings. Before entering, a sign sat outside of the restaurant welcoming George to his lunch. Buffalo Wild Wings was kind enough to donate lunch to all of us and placed pieces of George's favorite candy Snickers all over the table. George sat in front of me, and you could tell he was drained. It had been a long day for George. I was also tired, but I wasn't throwing the towel in until George threw the towel in too. Julie asked, "Do you want to end the day today? We can save your money and you can complete the shopping spree another time, if necessary. If you're feeling tired we can end it now." Looking at George you could see a part of him wanted to end it. He was having trouble eating that day, and the staff at Buffalo Wild Wings noticed he wasn't eating. They asked George if there's anything they could make for him off the menu. The waitress suggested a smoothie. George was tired, but nobody says no to a smoothie. Once George finished his smoothie, he asked if we could go to Macy's and call it a day. Julie told him if that's what you want, then of course.

We went to Macy's, George bought a few more things and the day was over. George had everything he wanted and his limo pulled around to the Macy's exit. The limo driver opened the trunk for us to put all of George's things in. The limo driver thanked us for doing what we do as wish grantors. He told us that we're doing a great thing. We told him that he is doing the same exact thing by staying with George all day and helping with his transportation. George and his mother both thanked us, and another wish was officially complete.

21

Make-A-Wish was still happy to have me back, and I started to sign up for more wishes. Looking at the newsletter every week, I continually signed up for wishes with boys between the ages of 10-17. I did this because that was my base. I wanted to continue do the same thing I did for Jerry and George. We would talk about sports or video games — the things boys were into, and with my help I would get him to his wish. I didn't want to expand my horizons. Because of my reason to just stay with one group, I didn't get any new wishes right away.

There are times when a wish grantor has an emergency and can't make it to a wish. For whatever reason, they signed up for a wish and now they can no longer do it. Changes do end up happening in life. I like to think I've proven that. I just happened to have the day off when the office called and asked if I could help a wish grantor that night. Seeing how I had struck out on wishes over the past month, I immediately said I'm available. The age and gender of child wasn't revealed.

I got in my car and drove to the address that the office sent to me. I wondered how this wish was going to go. Would the child like me? I put my car in park and chose to sit and wait in the family's driveway. A mother carrying a child came out from the house. I immediately got out of my car as I didn't want to be the guy who just randomly sits in someone's driveway without saying hello. The mother walked toward me and put her hand out and introduced herself. I said, "Hello." We exchanged the normal pleasantries during a conversation. She introduced her son whose name was Stan. Then she put down the child and told me the wish idea of a playset for her wish child. I was confused as I didn't know the age of the child or anything. She could've been holding the wish child or he could've been the little brother.

Eventually my second wish partner who I didn't know, Allyson pulled into the driveway. Allyson brought a toy truck for Stan to play with and he ran over to grab the car, and we watched him play in driveway with the truck. He would go through dirt and water with the truck. He even grinded the toy car on his mom's actual car. He was an incredibly happy kid with his toy car. I now knew he was the wish kid as no other child came to meet with us for the five minutes, we were outside. If I had to guess he had to be three years old. We could see that he loved to be outside. Stan's mom told us a playset would be the best idea for Stan and we knew he'd be thrilled with a playset as he loved playing. We said goodbye to Stan, and Allyson sent the paperwork back to the Make-A-Wish office. After working on three wishes. I never took on any major role. Outside of just communicating with those four stores before the mall wish, I never completed the paperwork or e-mailed the office during this time. I'm what they call an observer. I'll take a major role if I'm told I have to. I would say it's one of my faults. This wish required someone to help find the playset. I went to Google and found a website selling them and sent the link back to the foundation. My job was done, and it was now time to wait for the foundation to get the playset. I received an e-mail back stating "if you're comfortable would you like to call the store and ask about their prices?" I read the e-mail and thought, why me? I'm an introvert and I'm not a big fan of talking. It's a very relaxing and boring life. But it's safe. I like being safe. I thought, well we all need to grow up at some point and at 26 years old, I probably should. I e-mailed back with a confidant reply that I would call on my lunch break on Monday and it won't be a problem. I wondered, should I be taking on this responsibility? I am a just a volunteer after all. My Monday lunch break came, and I made the call. I had what the average person calls a conversation. Apparently, it's when people have a dialogue back and forth and they reach a conclusion that works for the both of them. Then they say goodbye. You should try it.

I contacted the foundation and they thanked me for making the phone call. I let the foundation take care of the pricing and everything was set. We eventually got to a date that worked for the family.

Volunteers from GE were due to help spread mulch during the day of the wish too. I thought before the big day that this may turn into something special. I asked my employer if I could take a half-day and they said sure. The day before, I told Stan's mother I had to work the entire day and I couldn't make it to the wish ceremony. She promised to send me a ton of pictures. I went into work that morning with my Make-A-Wish Volunteer shirt and waited. I e-mailed Stan's mother and asked her if she was excited to receive the playset. She said it had arrived and she was very excited as the delivery service placed and then assembled the playset that morning. I read that e-mail and couldn't wait to show up. I let my supervisor know when I was leaving, and I was ready. I was also planning on going to a local toy store to buy toys to put on Stan's playset. The time finally came as I checked my computer clock. I walked into the bathroom and changed into my Make-A-Wish volunteer t-shirt and walked to my car. I arrived at the toy store not knowing how many gifts I should buy or what my plan was. Luckily, because this wish was going to involve a major company like GE, people who work at the Make-A-Wish office in Trumbull were coming to the event. I called one of the office members and she said, "Buy whatever you think Stan will enjoy." While looking through the store, I remember seeing Stan play with toy cars so buying the toy cars was a must. I also got a few smaller items. I made the purchase, and I couldn't wait to get the house. I got on the highway and eventually pulled into Stan's driveway. As my car moved forward, I looked at the playset and I was amazed. Even though I was sent a picture of what that playset looked like by e-mail it was better to see in person. Maybe it was because I helped find the playset, or because I knew Stan would be really happy seeing it; I thought it was one of the greatest structures on earth. I really felt like it could compete for the greatest piece of architecture ever. I parked my car and walked to the door to see Stan's mother and surprise her. I didn't make it all the way to the door as she came out holding her daughter, and was shocked I was there. She laughed and was glad my job gave me the afternoon off. I honestly would've quit my job if I didn't get the afternoon off and couldn't witness Stan seeing his playset for the first time. Stan's mom told me to go walk around the playset and see how beautiful it is. I went to the top and looked out and thought, do I go down the slide to get down or do I climb back down like an adult? I realized this is Stan's playset and he deserves the first slide down. Also, I realized I was an adult. Kind of. I told Stan's mom it looks amazing. I almost forgot I brought toys for Stan. I went back to my car and grabbed the toys. I walked back up to the top of the playset and rested my bag of toys on top. As Stan's mom sat at the bottom of the slide anticipating this day to start, I asked if it was alright if I put the toys around the playset; that way it's like a little scavenger hunt for Stan and it's another element to his wish. She said she loved the idea, and I placed toys all over leaving some toys open and others closed, because I always felt like the joy of getting your own toys as kid is opening them yourselves too, or at least attempting to open them. Stan's mom sat at the bottom of the slide, and I stayed at the top for a few minutes waiting for time to pass. We were still hours away from Stan coming back to the house. The staff from GE was planning on coming a little later, so we needed to keep Stan away from the house for a little bit and that meant we needed to wait. The person I communicated with at the office, Kim Smith, pulled into

Stan's driveway with the Make-A-Wish logo on her car. I was still sitting on top of the slide pretending this was my new playset. Luckily in that moment I was enough of an adult to walk down the ladder and greet Kim. She was as amazed as I was by the playset. She greeted the mother and we talked about how nice the playset was. We waited for a bit and then Allyson pulled into the driveway. We exchanged pleasantries and she showed off the cake we were having with this celebration. A playset and a cake, what more could a little boy ask for? Another hour or so flew by, and then cars started to pull into the driveway. We realized it was the volunteers from GE coming to help with the wish. At one point so many cars were coming in it felt like we were in a parking lot at a concert. Eventually, Kim walked over and directed cars to park further on the lawn, and I had to move my car further up in the driveway so Stan's car could have a clear path in front of his playset. The GE volunteers started to get out of their cars, and they were amazed by the beautiful playset too. They all greeted the four of us still waiting for Stan's car to come in. The task for the GE volunteers was spreading mulch and creating signs for Stan to see as his car came down the driveway. Once they were giving the task, they went on their way and were a very well-organized machine. They knocked the project out within an hour or so. GE also bought special lights and sidewalk traction pads that stuck to the ground with paintings from employees on the front of every pad. The organization really went all out, and it was great to see. Now that everything was all set but we had to still wait for Stan. Also, the President of Make-A-Wish Connecticut, Pam Keough, came by to witness the wish reveal. It became one of those moments that you don't forget, and you want to write about in a book one day. GE finished mulching and the playset became a destination for Stan to enjoy. Stan's mom kept calling and asking where Stan was as his ride was attempting to keep him away while everything was getting ready. We finally got the message. Stan's mom told us he will be there in five minutes. The GE staff grabbed their signs and were told to line up on both sides of the driveway. I looked around and thought, what could I do? Stan's mom was holding a cell phone because she wanted to record this moment. She realized she couldn't do it and help Stan get out of the car. She asked, "Cory, could you film Stan?" I jokingly responded, "I don't know if I can handle that responsibility." Stan's mom felt like I could handle it and pushed her phone in front of my face. I grabbed the phone and she pointed toward the record button. "Once the door opens hit the record button." I took the phone and told Stan's mom I will do my best. Everyone stared up the road waiting for Stan's car to turn into the driveway. Finally, Stan's mom noticed the car and yelled, "That's him!" We all looked at the car and saw it coming toward the driveway. The GE volunteers screamed while holding up signs for Stan as the car came down the driveway. It was as if a celebrity was pulling down the driveway. And in a way there was. Stan was my celebrity. Finally, the car passed all of the screaming fans and pulled in front of the playset. I moved to the back seat of the passenger side door of my car and held the camera up. The driver came around and opened the door. That was the moment time froze for me. I saw his face for what felt like a few minutes. I can't remember if I hit the record button or not at the exact moment the door opened. There was this three-year-old child completely bald. I quickly thought, did he have hair that first day we visited him?

With my previous wishes, I never actually experienced seeing a child with no hair in person. With my previous wishes I was with kids who hadn't experienced hair loss. So, I never saw what these treatments do to a person, in person. You can watch videos and read all you want; until you see something in person you'll never truly know how to react. I knew I had to maintain myself for Stan and film this video. Once I realized that time is still moving, I held the camera and pressed record. Stan looked out of the car and he was afraid to exit. He would look out and then bury his head. Maybe he was tired, or he was afraid of the thirty random people who were in his backyard. Eventually, Stan's mom helped him out of the car and pointed him toward his playset. He saw it, and the race was on. I double- checked that the red light was on the camera and followed Stan as he ran toward the back of his playset and climbed the stairs. He was able to walk all the way to the top when he spotted the toys I put up there. He looked at them in amazement and started to play with them. The GE staff wondered what he was doing up there. I knew my toys were up there and that was our little secret as I overheard GE employees saying, "What's up there?" Eventually Stan played with all of the toys and came down the slide.

The greatest moment that came from the day wasn't actually granting his wish. It was the fact that no child came up to him and said, "What happened to your hair?" Nobody stopped him because of what happened to him.

We had cake and the wish was complete. Stan's mom thanked us and told us we could use her pool any time as a generous way of paying us back. I have yet to take her up on that offer. She also thanked me for showing up. I pulled out of the driveway and finally realized how great today truly was. On the car ride back the image of Stan without hair stuck into my brain. I did cry a little and punched my steering wheel a few times. I wondered why this happens to such young children? As those negative thoughts came into my mind, I had to remember the good of what was done that day with that boy running around his playset and enjoying the day. That's the message to remember; the greatness that comes with the foundation, not the reason kids are in it. If you just remember the negative then you can never change anything with the positive.

Then, an idea popped into mind: why not write a book? It seems pretty easy …

22

I started to think about how I would complete a book, so I just started writing. As I continued to write it became a major struggle. I spent my entire life watching television and playing video games and barely read a book for pleasure. Actually, I bought an Amazon Kindle and my dad jokingly said, "When do you read?" I ended up buying ten books on my Kindle in a four-year period. I also bought a Monopoly App on the Kindle. That app was used more compared to actual reading.

There was a small part of me that still wanted to be the hero of my own book, so I continued to write as I casually looked up ghostwriters on the internet. Knowing I still wanted to do this on my own and sending my health stories to a random person on the internet wasn't a great idea, I stopped looking. The internet is a powerful and useful device. But telling a random stranger to help me write about my recovery from lifesaving brain surgery isn't the best idea.

For a few months I kept writing on my own expecting this book to magically be written. The day they invent a magical pen that writes an entire book, please call me.

The next time I started to think about writing my book, I typed 'writing programs' into Google. Nothing came up of interest for writing programs, as I had no idea which programs were good or not. With that I went back to writing on my own.

Spending one day scrolling through my newsfeed on Facebook, I saw an ad for the Fairfield University MFA Creative Writing program. I clicked it because what can go wrong with clicking ads on the internet? A program overview came up. I didn't read any of it; I just knew I went to the high school on the Fairfield University campus, so I could trust this program. There was no wondering if this program was right for me or not.

I thought that my story is pretty unbelievable, and if any administrator at Fairfield University questions any of my stories, they can go down the street and check with the administration at Fairfield Prep. If I get in, that could be a newfound positive in spending four years at Fairfield Prep.

The requirement for the writing program was a twenty-page writing example and two recommendations. For the past year, I had been working on the memoir; that part was easy. I didn't touch the story up at all. If the program didn't accept how raw I was as a writer, then the program wasn't for me. My feelings on the program were that it would help shape me and make me a great writer. It was a college after all. Now I just needed two recommendations. My thinking was two; one from my employer and the other from Make-A-Wish Connecticut.

When it came to applying to sports job around Connecticut, I was too afraid to move away from Yale-New Haven Hospital. So, nothing came of it. No company wanted to hire me, which was frustrating as I was getting to an age when I had to start worrying about health insurance. Once I turned 26, I would have to have my own health insurance. If you've been reading this entire book and didn't just randomly flip to this page, you'll know the importance of me having health insurance. If you did just randomly flip to this page without knowing my need for health insurance, then you're reading this book wrong. If I never get sick again, could I grab a part-time job and attempt to climb the corporate ladder at a major sports company? Possibly. A different department where my dad works offered me a full-time job.

Knowing how important health insurance was, I accepted the opportunity at IUOE Local 478. I was slowly starting to lose interest in sports management, as I couldn't find a job in the field, so I wasn't that upset as taking a full-time job meant I was officially giving up on a job in sports management. In the end, I was being given a gift. Dorothy Siniscalchi gave me that gift. She was the first person I talked to about using ghostwriters for the book. If I was going to trust anyone to talk about my health and who I was as a person when I needed a recommendation, it would be her. She was kind enough to write a recommendation for me.

The second candidate I asked to get a recommendation from was Nicole Miles Conway. Nicole was the volunteer coordinator at Make-A-Wish Connecticut. She took over the job Cheryl held as she put out a list of new wish-eligible kids in an e-mail for all wish volunteers every Thursday. If anyone could vouch for the work I do at the foundation it would be her. She was happy to do it.

I sent the application in and got into the program. It was a great feeling to get into the program because I felt like I finally had a direction when it came to completing this book. Before I was going nowhere fast looking at random ghostwriters on the internet. But what had I signed up for? I didn't even know what an MFA in Creative Writing was.

I did a quick Google search and an article by a former professor in a MFA writing program appeared. The professor didn't name the school they taught at. I thought it would be nice to read about the positives of how a former employee at an MFA program felt. Instead, he wrote a hit piece. He pretty much stated MFA writing programs are pointless. They won't help you, and if you're just now learning to write at an older age, then the program won't work out for you. Without naming me directly in the article, he was telling me I was wasting my time. Now I had to worry if I making a huge mistake.

I didn't change my mind. Cory Metz doesn't quit; he finishes ideas he started. What if I quit on learning to walk again after the removal of spinal cord tumor? What if I quit after losing my memory after the brain tumor? Cory Metz doesn't quit after he gives his word.

I told my parents about the writing program. My dad likes being a guy who goes with the flow and never really thinks about the negative. He isn't a person who over-examines things. He thought it was a great idea. "If that's your passion go for it."

My mom on the other hand is an over-examiner and a worrier, and who could blame her? She did see her son cling for life in front of her eyes. She was by her son's side the entire time as she watched him have to rehabilitate his life twice. She didn't want anything bad to happen to her son, after everything he's been through. Which I get; being in the Foundation, I only want the best for the Make-A-Wish kids I worked with. With all they've been through, I just hope they're safe, happy, and healthy.

She questioned what I was doing with the same passion as the time, I told her David Wright failed to visit me in the middle of my wish trip. Do you member' that part of the book? (South Park)

"What are you doing?"

"Why?"

"What kind of program?"

"Are you sure?"

I answered every question with a straight face to a point where it seemed like I knew what I wanted from this program. I'm a pretty good actor when I want to be.

Because of my Oscar-worthy performance, she was convinced I knew what I was doing, and for a third time, I was going to college/university. My hope was that this time I could get what I wanted from a higher-education experience.

The Fairfield University writing program was on Enders Island, not the Fairfield University campus. That was my first mistake in a long list of things I failed to notice about the Fairfield University program.

The program being on Enders Island wasn't a major complainant as it was a beautiful place for a retreat. My parents drove me there, as they probably didn't believe that their son who didn't read or write his entire life got into a writing program at a university. Trust me I couldn't believe it either.

My parents helped set up my room on Enders Island and left me to fend for myself on the island. Like a fisherman all alone lost at sea.

I walked into the lobby where I got a schedule that stated a meeting would happen in the same spot at 5 PM. It wasn't something I was looking forward to. You know the whole meeting and interacting with people thing. That's not my scene. I went right back to my bed and waited till 5 PM.

5pm came and it was time to interact with people. I found a corner in the lobby and stood there. I stood there while every new face I didn't know walked through the lobby. You could just tell by looking at every face that all of these new faces were smart. Because of that I didn't attempt to hold a conversation with anyone. I didn't want to look stupid in front of any of these students. How can I be as good as these geniuses?

As I stood in the corner a couple of people came up to me and initiated conversations with me. Which was good, as ever since I was diagnosed my spinal cord tumor, I was afraid to interact with others. Talking about the real me had always been an issue. I'm glad someone came up to talk with me. Eventually the program director, Sonya Huber, walked to the center of the lobby and said, "Dinner is ready across the way."

Walking to the dining room with a group of intellectuals wasn't on my list of things to do on a winter night before I got into the writing program. Instead, I envisioned my time would be spent sitting on the couch watching sports, like I did all of my life.

The dining room had ten tables with ten seats at each. As I looked around, I could tell this room was very cliquey. It reminded me of my middle school lunch table. This time I was the outsider. I spotted some people were talking to each other, while others were just staring into their food waiting to leave. I liked the idea of the latter.

I spotted a table where a girl who came over to talk earlier was sitting. "Hey, we had a minute-long conversation before, do you mind if I sit here?" That'll be an easy conversation starter.

I walked over to the table and found a seat. "Can I sit here?" Five of the chairs were full with bodies and faces. All five faces looked me and either nodded their head or said yes. It was nice to see everyone being so inviting. Who knew just talking to people was so simple. At least that's how it was in the beginning.

The food was served, and a student walked next to me and asked, "Is anyone sitting here?" I shook my head no.

He recognized I was a new student and we started talking about what we're both doing in the program. I mentioned I am trying to write a memoir about being a Make-A-Wish kid and now a volunteer. He thought that was an interesting idea. As we ran out of things to talk about, he pointed to the girl I interacted with earlier in the day. "Do you know her?"

I looked at him and said, "Yeah, I had a quick conversation with her earlier."

"Just to let you know she's a member of Mensa."

I had no idea what Mensa was exactly; I had it assumed it was some club for smart people. I thought about countering with the fact I just won my fantasy football league in my office. I also wanted to discuss how I had the most points in the league. That's a serious accomplishment in my eyes. Before I opened my mouth, I thought, lets research what Mensa is exactly. If my dominant fantasy football year can compare to being in Mensa, I'll bring it up at the next dinner. Who doesn't like to talk fantasy football?

I finished my meal and immediately went to my room to look up what Mensa was. Mensa is basically a club for geniuses. As I started to read more and realized how smart you needed to be to get into Mensa, my reply of winning in fantasy football wouldn't match up. That conversation did change my spirit a little. How can I survive this? What am I doing here? Where's the door and can I leave now?

My parents and my brother sent me a text asking how it was going. As if I was solving some mystery on the island.

"It's fine. The girl I sat next to is in Mensa." My mom, who has four college degrees, asked, "What's that?"

I texted back that it's a club for geniuses.

My mom replied, "Oh." Then she asked my brother, "Did you know that?"

My brother replied yes. Of course he did.

The MFA writing program is broken down into two workshops. Before you go to the first workshop, you need to bring two writing samples with you and you need to read and review the work of the other writers in your workshop.

That was the first out of many writing mistakes I would make in the program. We were supposed to type up and edit everyone's writing sample. I didn't do that. I just read everyone's piece once through e-mail and failed to type any feedback or edits. Surprisingly the program didn't want me to just sit there and nod my head with every workshop assignment. That was a shame as I was pretty good at head nodding.

With that all three writing samples were work-shopped, and I just continually nodded my head. I wasn't going to make edits and print a review the day of. I messed up, and I had to accept the results of my mistake.

I tried to make statements during the workshop that would be helpful in any way. In all honesty I didn't know what to say. I re-read every writing sample on my laptop, and I didn't find any errors. They were well-written pieces and nothing seemed bad about them. All of it was just words combined together, forming a story. It looked fine to me. As someone who never wrote or read, how could I give good feedback anyway?

My sample came up and I managed to mess that up, too. We were supposed to submit work of our own that involved what we were working on. Obviously that meant me sending in work from my memoir.

For my first workshop I sent in a piece that had nothing to do with my memoir. It was so bad; I don't even want to discuss what it was about in this book.

My professor looked at and said, "What is this? This sample isn't why you're here is it?"

With embarrassment on my face, I responded, "No."

"I thought we were supposed to give two different writing samples. One can be from my memoir and the second something from a completely different idea."

My professor looked at me and said, "No. All of your workshop samples can come from the same book, they just can't be the same chapters."

I looked at the professor and the three other students like a fool and replied, "Oh."

Was that saying too much?

He looked back at me and in the nicest way possible ripped up what I wrote and told me, "I'm glad we solved that issue."

I smiled back. My smile held both embarrassment and happiness knowing I was slowly figuring out what this program was about. Barely.

And that's all I have to say about that. (Forest Gump)

My second workshop of the first semester went a little better, which wasn't saying much at all. I brought a workshop example from my actual memoir. It was the story of the playground wish. Six people including the professor were sitting in this workshop. The pressure was much higher at this point. As I knew I wanted a real opinion on this piece. An opinion I can actually use. Unlike last semester.

My writing example was fourth on the list to be workshopped. It was a cold winter that year, and although it was only ten degrees outside, inside our classroom I was starting to sweat as my writing example was coming up. Once again, the other writing samples were brilliantly done. And once again, I couldn't think of anything smart to say about the other samples. I would stare at random sentences and say, "I like how this sentence fits in the story; it really draws the reader in." Does that sound smart? Well, it didn't work well as the professor would ask for more of an explanation. I wouldn't have any more, and I would just sweat the time away and wait till the end of the session. It was like a terrible version of a sauna. Luckily, I faked it enough until it was time to have my sample broken down.

I smiled as everyone took my sample and started to have a conversation about it. There was a small part of me that felt bad as I never gave good advice to the other students in the workshop. That didn't seem fair, as I expected good advice from them. You know, tit for tat. (Clear History)

I only heard one word in their feedback. Expansion. I was told to talk more about myself. That feedback made perfect sense. It's an issue I've had all my life. Expanding and learning to talk more about myself. The issue grew even more once I was diagnosed with tumors on my body. The reader wants to know more about me. Hi reader. I just had one question for the professor. "Should I worry about making this book too geared toward adults? I want this book to be read by wish kids."

His response was "No. Just let the book flow the way you want. It doesn't need to be segmented toward anyone."

In the program, we would go to presentations by professors who had written and published books. I was amazed knowing that I was in the presence of someone who got their written word published into a book. To think words that a person thought of could be put into a book—and that book can be bought—was an accomplishment I believed to be impossible. During every presentation, I would sit alone and take in the words they said as they read from the books they published. Just being around writers was in a way enough for me.

The semester is always supposed to wrap up with a graduation ceremony for the students who got through the entire program. Although I struggled with my first workshop, I still wanted to be one of those students.

Unfortunately, the ceremony had to be cancelled because of a winter storm. I was mad about that, because I wanted to see the smiling faces of people who got to their goal in life and completed the program. Is there anything better than a graduation ceremony?

My dad picked me up and asked, "How was it?" I replied "Good." It was the concrete answer you'd expect from me at this point in the book. You would be happy to know I didn't disappoint.

My dad, who always disliked my one-word answers, asked, "What does that mean? What was good? Do you want to go back?"

In anger, as I've always hated expanding on my life, I replied, "I don't know, it was good. I took away a lot from the workshops. I didn't start off good, but it was very informative in terms of writing. I enjoyed it."

"Okay, do you want to go back?" "Yeah, I don't think I've taken away everything from the program. It's still a program that can help me."

We left the conversation at that, and I was officially a student of the MFA Creative Writing program at Fairfield University with my first workshop complete and starting my second workshop.

23

After realizing the importance of helping a much younger child, I signed up to help another child who was also three. I received a phone call from my fellow wish grantor David. His first question was, "How long have you been in the Foundation?"

"I've helped grant four wishes, and I was a wish kid in 2009."

His response was "That's great, when was your wish and what did you wish for?"

I told him my wish was 2009 and I went to the MLB All-Star game.

He then asked me a scary question. "Do you want to be the lead wish grantor?" The lead wish grantor is the person who is in constant communication with the wish family. He or she sets up the meetings with the family and responds to any questions the family may have.

I have yet to take this role on. I was still the person who feared calling about a playset. Before I said I was too afraid to take that role on, I thought back to my last wish. I remembered the conversation about the slide. Remembering that, I decided to be the lead wish grantor. I looked up the contact information for the wish child and called the mother. We had a conversation about what the Foundation does and what we're planning to do for her child. You could hear the joy in her voice, and we talked about the dates that worked for her family. My fellow wish grantor agreed to the date, and I had to let the mother know the good news. I called back and there was no answer. I looked on her wish sheet and saw she had three children under the age of five. A phone conversation probably isn't the easiest task for her. I texted her with the date we came up with and she agreed. Then she texted, "Thanks Cory! Looking forward to meeting you! And looking forward to doing something for my little guy."

I read that text and stared at that message for a few minutes. What do you tell a wish mother? I replied, "We will make it special. Just to let you know, I am a former wish kid and I've helped grant four wishes so far. You will have a lot to look forward to. The foundation does amazing work." She responded, "WOW! That is amazing. Happy to hear about happy endings. It's been a terrible year-and-a-half."

Our scheduled wish visit came a few weeks after my phone call. I pulled into Peter's driveway early. The kids and the father both spotted me. I got out of my car and told the father I was from Make-A-Wish. He shook my hand and said it was a pleasure to meet me. I replied, "Likewise," and I saw the wish child in the driveway. He was having fun playing with his sister and it didn't seem like he had a care in the world. It really felt like the exact same feeling I had with my last wish child. You would look at this child and say he has nothing wrong with him. He just looks like a normal kid playing with his sibling. The father told me to follow him and meet the child's mother. We walked over from the driveway to his house, and I said hi to the mother. You could see her joy knowing the fact her son was about to get a wish from the Make-A-Wish Foundation.

All three of us noticed a car parked in front of the house instead of the driveway. The father looked out the window and said, "It looks like someone else is here." I looked over and said, "Yeah that's the other wish grantor." I walked over to his car and greeted him. David had bought some toys for the kids to play with while the adults talked about the child's wish. The four adults took a seat and had a discussion about the foundation. The two parents had one idea in mind. It was to visit Walt Disney World. We didn't press the family, and we handed the family paperwork from the Foundation to sign. Every page was signed, and we said goodbye to the wish child as he kept playing with the toys that were brought to him. I laughed at the cuteness as he kept moving the truck up and down his floor. We said goodbye to the family and sent the paperwork off to the Foundation.

On the wish grantors Facebook page, a fellow wish grantor posted about having a Disney suitcase for a wish child. I wrote in the comment section that I have a wish child who's going to Disney. I imagined how happy the wish child would be with his suitcase while traveling through the airport before his wish. I was told the suitcase will be brought to the Make-A-Wish office. A week later the Foundation posted a picture of a Thomas the Tank Engine toy on the Facebook page. I texted the family and asked, "Does Peter enjoy Thomas the Tank Engine? The response was yes that he loves Thomas. I was the first in the comment section once again. The Thomas the Tank Engine train set was offered to my wish child. A response from the Foundation came with accepting the Thomas the Tank Engine toy. I assumed it would be as simple as having the two gifts sent to the Make-A-Wish child's house and we're done. I received a message from the office stating it was donated by a company and there's more to it. Because of this I needed to have a phone call with the foundation. I received a phone call from Kim Smith, and she told me about an event. She explained this event was similar to what happened with my previous wish child.

This event will once again be a different set of workers coming together to see the power of a wish. The only difference is this time the event will happen at their building. The day finally came for Peter to receive his Thomas the Tank Engine train set. I texted Peter's mom who was bringing Peter to the event and asked if she was ready for the event? She replied yes and thanked me. I told her that I don't know if the Foundation told you or not, but I can't make it to the event today. Please let me know how the event goes. She replied, no I didn't know you would've been there and I'll be sure to let you know how it goes. I thanked her and drove to the event. Why did I lie to a parent about not being able to go to an event for their child once again? I like telling people happy lies. What are happy lies? I define happy lies as lies that make you happy. A lie you hear and smile about. I like to see the shock and happiness on a person's face after I tell a happy lie.

I drove into the parking lot and looked for handicap parking in the visitor's section. I found the handicap parking spot and spotted the Make-A-Wish car in front of the entrance to the building. I opened my car door and shuffled with a sense of pride to the Make-A-Wish car, because I knew the sense of joy Peter will have while he's playing with Thomas. I walked to the car and Kim thanked me for coming to help. I acknowledged it wasn't a problem. Before we walked into the building, I was told we had to carry a couple of things in. The Make-A-Wish staff member told me she had a picture of the Make-A-Wish child. I grabbed it and it had been a couple of months since I saw Peter. I held the photo out in front of me. I looked down and saw his smile. I moved my eyes a little further up and saw a completely bald child. At first glance, I thought about handing the photo back and telling the Make-A-Wish staff member I can't do this again. For a second, I thought back to my last wish child. I thought back to me holding the cell phone and waiting for my wish child to see his playset. Holding the wish child's mother's cell phone as his mother picked him up out of his car seat caused so many emotions inside of my body. Waiting for a happy child to jump out of the car and run to his new playset. Instead, a bald child who was afraid to exit his car sat in the car. Can I face that sight once again?

A second later I remembered how excited that child was once he ran to his playset and the joy he got playing with the toys I got him. That was the moment to remember. I wasn't meant to remember the door opening and a bald child sitting in his car. I was meant to remember the child sliding down the slide. The boy playing with his friends as they ignored his bald head and just treated him like the neighborhood friend they always had. We were early and checked in with the front desk. Security gave us passes to travel up the elevator and into the ballroom at Anthem. As we walked toward our table, Kim asked if I was comfortable with giving a speech today? They thought that my being a Make-A-Wish kid and a wish grantor will help give the day another perspective. I agreed to the idea of giving a speech and found a table in the corner of the ballroom. I sat down for a couple of minutes and Kim came over to me and told me Peter was in the building. We stood by the elevator and waited for Peter to exit the elevator. I could've sworn in that moment it was 2009. I was re-living my All-Star game wish. It was just like my moment of anticipation where I waited to greet David Wright. This time I was waiting for a different superstar. The elevator opened and out came a mother and a child. I had a feeling it was the mother and child I knew. They walked through security, and it was the boy I met a couple months ago. The boy had the hair of an 80's rock star. He wasn't the bald boy in the photo. We walked into the auditorium, and I sat back at my table with Peter and his mother. I smiled and asked, "Are you surprised I'm here?" She laughed and said, "Yeah, I didn't think you would be here." We both laughed as employees from Anthem continually walked into the auditorium. I started to have a conversation with Peter's mother. She asked, "How many wishes have you worked on?" I told her I've worked on five wishes so far. I described what the other wishes were like and what the kids asked for. As I was describing what the other wishes were like, Peter was sitting in the chair moving up and down waiting for something to happen. In that moment he had the energy of ten kids his age. It was great to see. As I got to saying that the last wish, I worked on was getting a playset for a child, all of a sudden the mother started stroking her son's hair. I looked at the child's hair and thought his hair looked fine. Sure, I don't have a degree in hairdressing. But I can understand when a child's hair looks out of sorts. After I finished talking about all of the wish children I had helped, it hit me. I remembered the photo I was holding an hour earlier. The photo of her son smiling with a bald head. Her way of connecting with her son and forgetting about the tough times was looking and touching her son's full head of hair. As a mother she needed that hair back. She needed to reach out and touch it. For something that seemed so minimal it was incredibly memorable. We sat around for a few more minutes. Employees from the company would come over and talk to people at the table. At this point I'm pretty sure the wish child looked around enough times and spotted the large box on the table behind him. I could tell he was smart enough to know that box was for him. Kim Smith asked the mom if she was ready. She looked up and said, "Yeah whatever you need to me to do." The mom stood up with her son in hand and walked over to the microphone. I stayed at the table assuming I would be called over when it was my turn to give a speech. Kim took the microphone and thanked everyone for coming. She described the Foundation and thanked the company for inviting us. She looked at the Peter's mother and introduced her to the audience. I continued to sit and wait for an opportunity to stand and give my speech. The Peter's mother took the microphone and gave an incredible speech. She described what life has been like raising a sick child. As I heard her speech, my eyes started to tear up. I thought back to everything I went through and the sacrifices my mother made. The long days and nights in the hospital. In that moment I was the only person in the building who truly had a close understanding of what her words meant. I thought back to the day I asked my mom if I was still signed up for the basketball league. Or the day I woke up and I was unable to hold a conversation with my mother. As wish families, our lives are completely turned upside down in an instant.

The wish child's mother's speech ended, and I was still tearing up. I didn't attempt to walk toward the microphone. The world's greatest public speaker wouldn't have been able to follow her speech. Because of that I just stood away from the microphone and didn't bother to make a speech.

Kim grabbed the box and placed it in front of the Peter. Kim waved me over to help Peter open his giant box. I walked over and stood next to Peter and the giant box. Peter was staring at the box as if it was his birthday during the entire speech. Kim told him to rip the wrapping paper off the box. After he was done ripping the gift wrap off the Thomas the Tank Engine trainset, he was also handed the Disney suitcase. Next was the wish delivery party for the wish child. I had my party at Outback Steakhouse. I sent a text message to the mother asking what restaurants your family enjoys going to. She told me the family enjoys going to Chip's Family Restaurant. I knew the foundation had a connection to Chip's through our wish grantor's Facebook Page. I told Peter's mother that I would work my magic and get a reservation at Chip's. I contacted the Foundation and they got us a reservation. Some magic, right?

I needed to get sendoff gifts for Peter and his brother and sister. The incredibly memorable send-off gift I received was my T-Shirt with my sports hero David Wright on it. I had to create something that was of equal value. I actually sent a Facebook message to Georgianna for hints on where to buy wish delivery items as she would post create sendoff gifts she bought on Facebook. Georgianna suggested Walgreen's. I took a drive to Walgreen's in hopes of finding something Walt Disney-related. I was buying the sending-off gift around Easter; because of that, an Easter basket shaped like Mickey and Minnie was available. There were a few more Disney items I placed inside the basket and my shopping was complete.

The day of our Chip's visit came. I texted the family before our Chip's visit and she confirmed the family would be there. I entered Chip's and walked in with my Make-A-Wish hat and wish grantor t-shirt. The manager walked my way and said you must be with Make-A-Wish. "Yes, I am." "Is the number of people in your party eight?"

It may be nine. He acknowledged whatever the number is that it won't be a problem. I thanked him and waited for David my other wish grantor to show up at the restaurant. I stood outside of the restraint and within a minute I saw David's car We greeted each other with a hello and waited For Peter's family.

Peter's family pulled into the parking lot and we entered Chip's together. I sat directly across from Peter. After sitting for a couple of minutes my hero asked for Mac and Cheese. I think that's what the Avengers eat for lunch too. The staff at Chip's did a great job. In the middle of the meal, I took a sip of water and Peter's dad asked me, "What school are you going to again?"

I had texted Peter's mom and told her I was planning on writing a book about my health history, my Make-A-Wish experience, and being a wish grantor. I asked if it was okay to write about her son. She texted back of course, anything to help other kids. I told her that's the idea. I didn't think she told her husband about it.

I told him I was attending Fairfield University. Dan's grandmother came to the party as well. Peter's father said to Peter's grandmother, "He's trying to be a writer.!" I became embarrassed and started to describe the program and told them my hopes and dreams for the book. They were both impressed, and we continued to eat.

The meal came to an end and we said our goodbyes. Peter's grandmother and father wished me luck on the book as we exited. I told them I'll be sure to send them a copy. And the party was over. Peter was off to Walt Disney World for six days.

Once the trip was over and the family was back in Connecticut once again. I texted for one final time asking how was their trip. Her response was it was amazing. Once in a lifetime trip and we had an unbelievable time.

24

I just moved to North Haven to be closer to my full-time job, and one of my dad's former co-workers, Dan Krause was a member of an Italian club in North Haven. My dad told me to see what the club is all about so I can network with people in town. Out of curiosity, I went. I wore my Make-A-Wish hat; I thought it could be a conversation starter with somebody in the club. Who doesn't love talking about the Foundation? My dad's former co-worker's wife, Denise was a member of the board. She sat at the front table through the entire meeting. The meeting hadn't started and all of the sudden ten minutes into my being at the meeting, a person started having a conversation with her. I looked out of the corner out of my eye, and it looked like they were pointing at me and talking about me. I thought nothing of it and focused my attention elsewhere. All of a sudden this person came walking behind me and tapped me on the shoulder. She spotted my hat and asked, "How do you know Make-A-Wish Connecticut?" I replied, "I'm a wish granter." She looked at me and moved my hat up to see my face. "Cory." I looked up and acknowledged her use of my name. I've put things on Facebook before, so I thought it was entirely possible people know my name and I wouldn't necessarily recognize them back. She saw my confusion and stated, "It's Georgianna."

In case your memory isn't very good like mine, Georgianna was the person who granted my wish in 2009. Georgianna messaged me through Facebook, and we planned on working on granting a wish together. Georgianna and I worked on a new wish for a boy named Kyle. She called the family and arranged a date to visit.

I drove to Kyle's house and texted Georgianna indicating I was there. She texted back that she was there too parked across the way.

We walked to Kyle's house together; it was strange, as it was eight years ago I was the boy on the other side of the door waiting for her to enter my house. It's funny how things can change in life.

The door opened, and Kyle's mother smiled. She waved us in, and I spotted Kyle. He was running around the house like the Energizer Bunny. He kept going and going—which was nice to see—as I know I have my days where my energy is drained, and I just want to lay on the couch all day.

At the kitchen table, Georgianna took out her paperwork while Kyle continued to run around with a balloon that Georgianna brought for him. Kyle's mom said, "The best idea for Kyle is to visit Disney. He loves Mickey, and I think he'll enjoy his time there." Georgianna did the paperwork and we left the house.

We had Kyle's wish delivery party at the Olive Garden. Georgianna and I carpooled together, and I thought about how many people have done what am I doing. A wish child who had their wish granted and then granted two wishes with both of their wish grantors. I was most likely on a very short list to ever accomplish that.

We arrived early and found our reserved table, and the staff couldn't have been more generous, as they continually made sure we were comfortable throughout the entire dinner.

Georgianna attached balloons to the chairs around the table, as we knew balloons were Kyle's favorite things.

Waiting for Kyle brought me back to my wish delivery at Outback. I remember the happiness that came with going to my favorite restaurant. I hope Kyle the same feeling of enthusiasm I had.

Kyle and his family arrived and walked to our table. All of them looked happy and had a smile, except Kyle. Kyle wasn't the same child I saw at his house. He looked tired as he sat at his table and didn't react to much as Georgianna and I attempted to interact with him. Was he falling into the sick-kid trap I battled with my entire life? At that point Georgianna had completed over two hundred and fifty wishes in the Foundation; if anyone is going to help Kyle feel better it would be her.

Georgianna looked at Kyle and said, "We got presents for your trip to Disney. Do you want to see them?" Once that statement was made, I saw one of the largest smiles I've ever seen in my life. I knew the 'happy Kyle' was always there; he just needed to know about the power of the wish to bring that happiness out. Georgianna pulled out every Disney toy you could imagine and Kyle continued his smile for the rest of the dinner.

We left Olive Garden and wished Kyle and his family well as they were off to Disney.

During their trip Kyle's mom texted me photos of the memories Kyle was making. I appreciated seeing Kyle's smile once again.

After the wish trip, Kyle's mom texted me to have a meeting. I found it strange, as I never had a meeting after the wish. I experienced Kyle's wish through text and knew everything that happened. We weren't living in a time before cell phones. This wasn't the 90's, where I needed to look at developed film from Kyle's wish to understand how his trip went. But I never say no to wish families and told her a date and time that worked for me.

We met at Panera Bread and Kyle's mom said, "We wanted to thank you for the work you did granting Kyle's wish." She handed me a bag. I looked at and didn't know if it was appropriate to open in front of her. I asked, "Is it okay if I open it here?" She replied, "Yes."

First, I saw and read the card inside. On the front page the card said, 'those who give of their time are truly generous.' That was nice to read.

The inside of the card said, 'just saying "thank you" doesn't seem enough. I hope you know how appreciated you really are.' A personal note said, 'Hope this little note continues to encourage the goodness of your heart.'

I also received a Walt Disney World coffee mug and a Give Kids the World hat. Give Kids the World is the resort wish kids stay at. It's an unbelievable place, I wouldn't be able to detail all of it in this book. Please look on the internet and seek it out yourself. I'm telling you this story because it speaks to how great Kyle's family is. To think of me while enjoying their wish experience truly speaks volumes.

☐

25

After helping to grant wishes for boys for the past six years, I figured it's time for something new. It's time to bring some girl power to my work with the Make-A-Wish Foundation. I signed up to help 11-year-old named Ariel.

I guess my fear in helping a girl would be the same idea as helping a child who's three years old. I have zero relatability to an 11-year-old girl. I always envisioned my work with the Foundation as being able to relate to the wish child. I can bring up sports, video games, and television to a wish child. Those three things got me to my wish. Do 11-year-old girls enjoy those things, too? Being a different gender, I always thought I haven't had her experiences to truly understand what she would want as a wish child. I couldn't possibly help her get to her wish. I was wrong.

I set up a phone call with my new wish grantor, Pat Harriman. During our conversation Pat asked, "How long have you been volunteering with the Foundation?"

I replied that I've been with the Foundation on and off between school for five years. I was a wish kid in 2009. She was shocked she had yet to meet or know my story as a wish kid. My story as a former wish kid had moved around the Foundation for the past few years because I had posted a few things on our wish-grantors Facebook page talking about how much it means to be a former wish kid and now a wish grantor. Pat had yet to hear my story, and I told her about how I went to the 2009 MLB All-Star Game. I told her I met all of the players in the game and former president Barack Obama. She paused on the phone for a second. She said the fact that was all in one wish was very impressive.

Pat volunteered to make the phone call to the family, and I told her I would grab the icebreaker gifts for Ariel and her brother. Buying the icebreaker gifts is always a new and fun experience with every new wish. Although I've been told I had to find gifts for Ariel, who was eleven, and her brother who was nine. I texted Ariel's mom for ideas as I had no idea what to get and was told Ariel likes Harry Potter, Wonder Woman/comic books, and dogs. Her brother likes science, animals, comic books, and Legos. They both also enjoy the outdoors. How should I work with that? Do I buy a dog that wears glasses and put the dog in a Wonder Woman outfit? The dog would be called Wonder Potter. The dog's superpower is barking and wanting to go outside. Is that creative? For the brother I could get another dog and put him in a Superman outfit. Yeah, that's it. I sent a Facebook message to Pat and asked, "How much money can I spend for the icebreaker gifts?" She replied, "Under twenty-five dollars for both children." Dogs are expensive and for good reason as they're the greatest companion a person can have. I continued to think of ideas and went to a local Paper Store near my house.

The store had greeting cards in the middle, while toys and books stood to the sides of the store. I walked to the right of the store where I spotted some toys. One toy jumped out to me in particular. The toy was called the Dinosaur Dome. I grabbed the box and read it thoroughly as if I was back to holding the ambulance truck at Hobbytown U.S.A. Studying the box, I saw the tagline for Dinosaur Dome is 'to create your own dinosaur domain! Comes with your own pet dinosaur! Excavate a stunning dinosaur fossil! Grow real prehistoric plants! Watch a dinosaur plant grow in hours.' I thought about buying my own box for myself, too. I was starting to come around myself. I've never been able to grow my real prehistoric plants in my twenty-seven years of life. This would be my first opportunity to see and feel real prehistoric plants. As I flipped the box over, I saw it was on sale and would fit into the under twenty-five dollar price range. Next, I walked to the other side of the store to look at the books and spotted one named Really Important Stuff My Dog Has Taught Me. I grabbed the book and thought it's a must-buy, since I'm killing two birds with one stone. I'll be buying a book with Ariel being an avid reader she will love that. Also, it's about dogs, and she loves dogs. I bought the two items and left with a sense of pride knowing I had succeeded in finding two gifts for the brother and sister. After that, I had a feeling working this wish would be a great experience.

It was a beautiful day in May and Pat coordinated the date to meet Ariel. I made my traditional early arrival and pulled in front of Ariel's house.

As I pulled alongside the house, I spotted a large dog staring directly at me from inside the house. I thought, 'phew better to have the dog than having a wish child, mother, father, or family member come outside and ask me what I was doing in front of their house?'

As cars continued to drive by, I would continue to think, is that Pat? No. Next car drives by. Is that her? No. A car pulled into the driveway and then backed out to pull in front of me. That's Pat.

In unison, we both exited our cars and said hello to each other. We shook hands and walked toward the door together. I took in a deep breath and knew on the other side of the door that there was a child who could use my guidance.

The large dog continued to stare as Pat rang the doorbell. All of a sudden, the mother came to the door holding the dog. She opened the door and told us both to please come in. The both of us walked in with a smile.

Pat walked in first and said hello to Ariel. I was still being blocked by Ariel's mom and didn't look at Ariel at the same time as Pat did. A few thoughts scrolled through my mind before seeing Ariel. Will I be able to help Ariel get to her true wish? Will she even care enough to hear my help?

As I thought about picking a new wish, I truly sat and thought about helping those two three-year-olds. What made those wishes so special was the uniqueness. Sure, continually repeating Jerry's wish of creating ideal sports wishes would've been simple and easy. But, in life it's okay to be different and to be challenged. If anyone should understand challenges it should be me.

We walked toward the kitchen table and Pat placed all of the paperwork on the table. She looked at me and said, "Cory has some gifts for you and your brother." I handed the gifts over and both kids had smiles. Pat looked at Ariel and asked if she had her notes with her. I looked at Pat with confusion. What notes? Will there be a test next?

This was a new idea that was recently implemented by the Foundation; that way a kid can have wish ideas written out before wish grantors meet with them. I took a strong interest in what her wish was as I loved seeing new ideas the Foundation came up with.

To start she had a few post-it notes in front of her. We went one-by-one and continually eliminated ideas. She would put a post-it note in front of Ariel and ask, "Why do you like this?" And then that would be compared to other notes. We got to a point where three notes were left, and it was clearly becoming a struggle for Ariel.

Ariel was starting to look toward her mom in hopes she would answer the question, "What should my wish be?"

Once I saw that, I knew I had a purpose here. I spoke up by saying, "I'm a former wish kid, and my advice is to think of the one thing that was always on your mind while you were in the hospital. The one thing that defines who you are." That advice is true for all wish kids.

Ariel's mom said, "That's good advice, and what was your wish?" I replied, "I loved sports and I picked the baseball All-Star Game." Ariel came up with her wish idea after I made that comment.

Now I know this will seem like a total cop out. And in a way it is. But I'm going to stop here and not tell you anymore information about Ariel's wish. I'm doing this because I told Ariel that one day, I want her to write her own memoir. She is such a prolific reader, and I know she has a story to tell. So I won't be telling you anything about her wish as it's her story to tell. I'll just say her real name is Charlie Elliott, and I can't wait to read her book.

26

Sure, my first workshop didn't start off well. When you have a learning disability it's tough to get things in order. That's where I placed the blame for my failure in my first workshop.

Now the actual semester of school was officially starting and my faculty advisor for my first semester was Rachel Basch. She was very nice and helpful as an advisor. I don't know what happened in terms of my ability to comprehend school. It could be the fact I had to maintain a full-time job this time or the program was too tough for me.

During my first phone call after attempting one assignment, I casually mentioned to Rachel that I had a learning disability, and it may take me longer to complete assignments. I asked, "Could I get more time for assignments?"

She replied, "Yes, I'll give you the assignments earlier." That was helpful as I wasn't planning on giving up on the program because of my disability.

We were told to write craft essays on each book we read. We had to read ten books and write craft essays on each book. I didn't have an issue with reading books. Although I hadn't read books my entire life, I believed I could pick up on reading quickly. Although, I'd rather binge-watch the latest show on Netflix. Are you watching Big Mouth? Now that's a well-written show.

It was the craft essay that I couldn't wrap my head around. If I had to give you a definition, I'm pretty sure you pick an element of writing first, then you describe how that element is used in the book. Pretty sure that's it.

The phone calls kept happening and the craft essays continued to be an issue. I ended up getting through the semester, but in no way was my work at the level I wanted it to be, or that it should be. But I was still happy I was making the attempt. Considering what I have been through. That's something.

The next workshop came, and this time it was in the summer. I had a better idea of what this program was about. I brought the stories of George's wish trip to the mall and I brought Jerry's wish to the workshop. I was barely a little more organized this time.

This time, being summer, I assumed it would be a little easier to be open and hold conversations with others. You know, be a normal person. I brought two cornhole boards and bags with me to make friends through cornhole. People do it at tailgate parties, why not a writing program?

I was about to grab the board, and then I spotted groups of random people who weren't in the writing program walking around the island. It was clear in the summer the island wasn't reserved for Fairfield University students. Knowing that I wasn't entirely confident in leaving my cornhole boards outside, I left them in mom's car, and she drove back to Fairfield.

When I grabbed my room key for the week, I was told there was a meet and greet at the tent across from our rooms. After I was told about the tent, I thought about my last meet and greet over the winter. Thinking about how incredibly awkward that was, I choose to do the childish thing and stay in my room. Why, you ask? My simple answer is because I didn't want to deal with looking like a fool again. I just wanted to be left alone. My disability overtook me once again.

My first workshop was with Eugenia Kim. The workshop piece I brought was the mall wish. I liked to think it was similar to the playset wish sample. I just hoped we can have long conversations about the piece.

We didn't. I was told they want to hear more about Cory. Again, I thought I did my best. Once again, I came up with nonsense answers to the other samples from the other students. I didn't say anything noteworthy. I created different buzzwords to make it seem like I knew what I was talking about. "I like the sentence structure here." Words that I believed my fellow students wanted to hear. Kind of like today's politicians. I'll walk myself out.

It was a pretty underwhelming workshop. I kept a smile on my face and got to the end of it. After the first workshop of the summer, a writer named Andre Dubus came to speak with us. He spoke about his book as it was the common read for all students. The common read is a book assigned to all the students in the program. The writer comes to the island, and the students and the writer have an open discussion about their book.

He thanked all of us for reading his book and stated, "Thanks for having me and I think it's great to have so many creative writers in one space."

He then said that in these public speaking situations that he enjoys open discussion. The discussion starts with students talking about characters and what they like or don't like in the story. I chose to sit and say nothing. It's what I do best. In all honesty I thought his book was a just story and people couldn't possibly discuss. It was a good read but I had no reason to discuss it. I'm sure he did his best, but having an open discussion about characters seemed useless in my mind. I guess that's what people who read enjoy to do.

After the book discussion we had dinner. I found a table with zero bodies around it and sat down. Eventually people started to fill the table as the room was getting full, and wouldn't you know it, Andre Dubus asked me, "Is anyone sitting here?" I froze up a little; it was similar to my Derek Jeter interaction in not knowing what to say. I was just amazed I was in the midst of a real writer. He accomplished what I was attempting to accomplish by being in this program. Sitting to the left of him, Bill Patrick, the man who in the nicest way possible ripped up my first writing sample, had also asked to sit at the table.

Andre went around the table asking what everyone was up to. The two people to my right spoke up about their projects. I couldn't remember what they said because I was thinking about the question, what am I up to? I honestly don't know what I am up to. I know I'm struggling with this writing program. I know I'm attempting to write a memoir. That's about all I know. The voices of the two people to my right shuttered, and it was my time to speak.

I froze up. This moment reminded me of Peter's grandma asking me about the writing program. And wouldn't you know it, I had a glass of water in my hand just like I did when I was talking to Dan's grandma. I took a gulp of water and got ready to say something.

Before I could utter something incompetent to an author, Bill stated, "Cory is working on a great idea for a memoir. Wait till you hear about it."

"Oh, really? What are you working on?"

I appreciated Bill opening the door for a conversation. "I'm a former Make-A-Wish child, and now I grant wishes for Make-A-Wish children."

"That sounds very interesting. And what was your wish?"

With a smile, I told him, "My wish was to go to the 2009 MLB All-Star Game."

Bill looked over and said, "And who did you meet during your trip?"

I replied, "Billy Bob Thornton."

Did you almost believe me?

I seriously replied, "Barack Obama."

His final statement meant a lot to me as he said, "That's great, keep working on it, and I can't wait to read it in the future."

My second workshop was awful. By this time, I had to finally admit to myself that what I was doing in this program was awful.

Six students including the professor sat and stared as we decided the order for our samples to be read. My sample would be fifth.

Two samples were read the first day. With both samples it was business as usual for me in terms of saying nothing. Once again, I could see the disappointment in the students and the professor as no words were uttered from my mouth. I walked back to my room in hopes that maybe tomorrow would be better. In what way it could be better, I had no idea.

The next day two writing samples came and went. I did the same thing in terms of not talking. The frustration from everyone was clearly growing. I was clearly failing in this program.

I grabbed my notebook and backpack with minor disgust. I walked back to my room, and my professor from that workshop happened to be trailing behind me. She stood next to me and casually mentioned, "Hey, try your best to get in the conversation. No matter what it is just add to the conversation." I looked at her and nodded, I got back to my room and just sat alone on my bed.

I was a little defeated by the conversation. I knew that I wasn't succeeding in the workshop; it just hurt to hear from a professor directly. Nobody wants to be openly criticized by someone. As I sat in somberness waiting for dinner, I received a text from Ariel's mom.

There are times the Foundation gets donations from fantastic people or organizations around Connecticut for tickets to major events. Ariel and her mom ended up getting tickets for a Taylor Swift concert! I asked for photos from the concert, as wish grantors post photos and videos of wish kids on our private Facebook page.

Ariel's mom ended up sending me a video of Ariel with text underneath it saying, 'I've never seen Ariel so happy. Thank you."

I clicked on the video, and I heard singing in the background. Then Taylor Swift as well as Ariel sang, "I don't care, I love it."

For my entire life I've listened to rock music. My favorite bands are Nirvana, Motorhead, and Twisted Sister. I never listened to Taylor Swift. Ever since that song was released, I did my best to avoid it. As a fan of rock music, I found it to be very annoying. But hearing Ariel or I guess I can say Charlotte sing those words, I cried.

The tears came because I knew what singing those words meant. Maybe this is a writer reading way too much into lyrics. But I heard those words and thought there was a much deeper meaning into the way she sang it. "I don't care, I love it." She was saying, 'I don't care about my past health history; none of it matters. I don't care.' When she says 'I love it,' she is saying I love life. The past is the past, and she is living and loving the life she's living now. After seeing that video, I knew I couldn't give up on my story.

The next day, my piece was workshopped, and I awaited people to comment on my piece. Everyone looked around not wanting to be the first one to comment. The expression, you could hear a pin drop, would have been obligatory in this situation.

Eventually someone said, "I like the idea. The Jennifer Lawerence story is funny." Then flat out a student said, "There were a lot of grammar mistakes, and it needed expansion everywhere." In the back of my mind, Ariel's voice singing I don't care, I love it showed up. Thinking about that video, I knew I had to take the constructive criticism and never give up. Instead of lashing out at the criticism, I swallowed my tongue and said, "Thanks."

I tried my best to comment on the last piece during the last workshop, but as you can imagine, I failed at that miserably. I did do one thing correctly during that week. That one thing was the student readings. The student readings were a time at night when any student could go up for two minutes and read anything they were was working on. I thought that me having that Billy Bob Thornton moment would be a great story to read. This time I was going first. Last semester I attempted to read my Billy Bob Thornton, but I didn't sign up in time. They save the best for first.

It was a good thing I was going the second, semester as this time I was prepared with the prop of having the autograph pad.

My name was announced by the person who told me the girl sitting next to me was in Mensa. I forgot his introduction as he gave funny introductions to every person who came up to read. If I had to guess it would've been something about how this is the quietest person in this program's history and for some unknown reason, he wants to read. Here he is Cory Metz. Whatever it was I told the story and it worked out well. I held up my autograph book and everyone laughed. After that people were starting to accept to me and I started to do better socially.

Being the summer, this time I got to see the students graduate without a winter storm taking that away. It was exciting to see happy faces get their diplomas. After succeeding at the student readings a very small part of me thought that could be me.

There was a graduation party in the tent after everyone received their diploma. I didn't go. I just walked back to my room and stayed in my room alone. I was having conversations with people at dinner now; I was doing better. Maybe subconsciously, I was struggling so badly at the workshops and I remember that first meeting in the lobby and standing there like an idiot for two hours caused me to not repeat that performance on the grand scale of a graduation party, thus forcing me to walk back to my room instead of the party. I don't know. I just wanted to be left alone.

The next day we got faculty advisors, and I was assigned to Eugenia Kim. Out of all of the professors I worked with in the program, she admired what I was doing with Make-A-Wish the most. She told me to make sure I can use the Make-A-Wish name when writing this book. I e-mailed the office, and I had a phone call scheduled for later in the week.

We had a meeting to map out what I need to do for the next semester. The meeting took place at a table looking out to the ocean. I thought about how I could get used to this. Eugenia handed me a sheet with a list of books on it and asked, "Cory, what do you like to read?"

I looked back at her with a glazed look thinking, what did she just ask me? What do I like to read? I do a good job of reading fantasy football stats, that's about it. Before that grossly incompetent answer was sputtered, I said, "I don't read."

She looked back at me as if no student had ever uttered something so vile and disgusting on the island. With that response I could've sworn someone would've taken me away in handcuffs and banished me from ever visiting the island. Or I would've been thrown into the ocean to never be seen again.

She replied with some hesitation, "Okay, let me pick some books out for you to read this semester." She ended up circling ten books for the semester and told me to write ten craft essays on the books and five 20-page pieces from your memoir. I looked back and thought with zero hesitation that it will be no problem.

My dad picked me up, and I told him it went better this time. I told him about how my Billy Bob Thornton story got a lot of laughs. "What Billy Bob Thornton story?"

I told my dad the story and he laughed. That was in fact the greatest accomplishment of the past ten days. He said, "That's a pretty good story."

☐

27

I did my best to send Eugenia work, and I will be the first to admit my work was awful. You can't rush writing and that's what was happening. Eugenia was nice enough to string me along for two pieces. By the third piece she finally said something.

I can't remember how she phrased it exactly, but she pretty much told me to think about leaving the program. She spotted that my work wasn't improving and that these packets are just being rushed.

I ignored her conversation and assumed I was doing fine. I knew I wanted to write about the Fairfield University writing program in my memoir. I wasn't going to write about how I dropped out of the program. What kind of message is that to wish kids? If something gets tough quit? No, I won't allow that.

I told my mom, "I think I was just told to leave the program." My mom replied, "Do you think, you should leave?" "No, I replied."

I chose to carry on with the program, and then all of a sudden I started to get unbearable neck pain. It became so bad I couldn't even attempt to move my neck without pain. I was leaving work during lunch to sleep at my house. Sometimes I would fall asleep and be so tired I would text my boss saying I'm too tired to make it back to the office. Any pain in my neck and sleeping more than usual could mean something. I didn't think much of it until the pain was bad enough where I would go into my bed and bury my head in my pillow. That's when I started to realize this was very similar to when my brain tumor was discovered. By the third time I repeated this same process, I texted my mom and she replied, 'I'm calling the doctor.'

My only thought in that moment was, no. If a phone call happens that means I'll probably have to go the hospital and get a MRI and then who knows what I'll be told. I took the next logical step by burying my head in my pillows and wishing for the neck pain to magically disappear.

This time I got a phone call back from my mom. "Dr. Baehring's office wants you to go visit the emergency room." Are you serious, the emergency room? It was just neck pain, it'll go away.

As I thought about that statement it just sounded senseless in my mind. Did I not remember what 2008 was like? I almost lost my life because we didn't find where the painful headaches were coming from. If the doctor wants you to go visit the emergency room, then visit the emergency room.

A co-worker, Tiana Ocasio, spotted how bad I looked and made sure I got home and asked me how I was feeling. I told her I was going to the emergency room. My mom was coming from Fairfield to bring me. She responded by saying, "I'll bring you." I was amazed by her generosity and took her up on the offer as my mom was about a half-hour away.

On the car ride there, I continually thanked her for the ride and she continually said that it was no problem. It wasn't the greatest conversation ever, but what conversation to the emergency room has ever been great?

She pulled into the emergency entrance and offered to stay. I politely declined as I wasn't a kid anymore and needed to start handling this medical stuff on my own.

She told me to call if anything comes up. If anything comes up? Let's hope nothing comes up. I walked or limped(however you'd like to define my walking) and told the front desk, "My name is Cory Metz, Dr. Baehring told me to come and get checked out." She looked back at me and said "Ok. Let's just check your vitals and then we'll bring you back."

My vitals were checked and they were normal, which was the only normal thing about my body. I was then brought to a corner room in the emergency room with a bed and a television. I was asked about the issue and gave the most logical response I could think of.

"I can't move my neck, because it's incredibly painful." The Yale staff member took note of that comment and replied "Ok. I will be in contact with Dr. Baehring and we'll go from there. Rest for a bit until we hear from Dr. Baehring directly."

I immediately relaxed by looking up at the television, which is what I do best, and put on Comedy Central. It was the most important day of the week. South Park marathon day! I started to forget about my neck pain and laughed as I got lost in the latest episode.

My mom showed up wondering how I was laughing at this moment. In what way could any of this be funny? I pointed to the television indicating South Park was on. She laughed too, as she was relieved I wasn't losing my mind.

My dad, who had been traveling around the state of Connecticut, came to the emergency room and asked, "You alright?" I responded, "Yeah." We're a very conversational pair.

A member of Dr. Baehring's team came to talk with me. "Hi Cory, I just had a conversation with Dr. Baering, and he believes you need a MRI. Dr. Baehring mentioned how you never complain about pain. For you to complain today may mean something is acting up in your body."

By 7 PM I was taken from the emergency room up to a double room. I was told the MRI machine would be available later in the night. What a day.

The South Park marathon was still playing until the new episode started at 10, and I could take small solace in that.

9:30 came and I was told it was time for my MRI. Now I was going to miss the new episode of South Park. Would it have been appropriate to ask for a re-schedule time because of a new South Park episode being on? Probably. I still thought about it though.

I left my glasses in my room, as I didn't need them for a MRI. There's never been anything good to look at in a MRI machine anyway. With my glasses off, I was on my way to face the dreaded MRI machine once again—the machine that started this entire story. My body was picked off my bed and placed into the MRI machine for two-and-a-half hours.

The same noises I heard in the machine all those years ago rang through my ears. I became a conductor in my mind as I knew how long the next ring would be and when it would end. I was a conductor performing in front of no one. This must be how Mozart felt. How's that for a reference? By hour two my body started to struggle, and my legs began to jump.

Before my MRIs, I take a pill that relaxes my body and calms me down. Because my MRI was happening so quickly, I couldn't get the pill in time.

As the MRI technician let me out of the cocoon from hell that is an MRI machine, I started to have the 'Why me?' thoughts. I was brought to a holding area to wait for someone to transfer me back to my room. When I was being moved, I said to myself, why am I here? It's 12:00 AM, I should be in my bed getting ready for work. Once that thought popped into my head, I heard a voice of a child.

I didn't have my glasses, so I couldn't identify the age of the voice. All I could identify was a child's voice, and he was talking with his father. I heard that voice and knew I had to stop my thinking. There was a boy who at the stroke of midnight was going in for a MRI. I had to stop my thinking. Remember that kid was you once.

Back in my room, a second patient had moved in. Something I hated to see in my room as my want to be alone was being disturbed by this man sleeping a bed away from me.

This man was the loudest snorer I had ever heard in my life, thus causing me to stay awake for the entire night. What's there to do when one can sleep? You can write, and that's what I did.

I posted this on a private Facebook page for wish grantors in the Make-A-Wish Foundation:

"Hello fellow wish grantors,

Yesterday I was admitted into the hospital, because I was suffering from severe neck pain for the past five days. Some of you know this and others don't: the reason I was a wish kid in 2009 was because of a brain tumor. I have yet to have any radiation treatment because my tumor cells are in a position where 50% of doctors will say to get treatment, while the other 50% will say to just watch the cells. I am with a doctor who says just watch. I have been watching for nine-and-a-half years of my life, and any sign of random pain for an extended amount of time near my brain can possibly mean something is wrong with my brain shunt or that the tumor cells are attacking my brain in vulnerable areas. And that could trigger a seizure or something much worse.

Last night from 10:00 until 12:30 AM, I was lying inside an MRI machine resting my eyes as best I could. Believe it or not, for the majority of the time I laid in that machine, I thought about the Make-A-Wish Foundation. I thought about wishes I've granted and how special those kids are. Keeping those kids in my mind helped get me to the end of the test.

I'll be honest. If there was a way I could switch bodies with a body that had none of the health concerns I suffer from, I would think about switching tomorrow. I say that because for the rest of my life, the slightest neck pain, back pain, or headache can lead me into a hospital bed as it did last night, and truthfully, that's not a fair life to live for anyone. I wouldn't wish any of this on my worst enemy.

And yet my life is amazing in it's own way because of the body I have. I volunteer with the greatest charity organization on the planet and have meet some of the strongest kids and families on this planet. That perfectly healthy Cory Metz body would pale in comparison to the former wish kid Cory Metz that you know today. The perfectly healthy Cory Metz body wouldn't be able to go up to a Make-A-Wish kid and say "I understand what you went through and I'm here to help" as I am able to do today.

Finally, I am currently in a writing program at Fairfield University and working on writing a memoir. It's the toughest thing I've ever done. Much tougher than learning to walk again as I did after my spinal cord tumor removal surgery or re-training my brain as I lost a majority of my memory in 2009. All I ask is one favor from everyone here. Please give me encouragement to get to the end of this book. I have moments of writer's block where I feel like throwing my laptop out the window or tearing apart the books the program assigned me. If you can send me a message telling me about a wish kid you have or had, as I get closer to my goal. The idea of the book is that I'm writing the book I never had once my health struggles started. I know there's a child sitting in a hospital bed at this moment looking for an outlet. Something that let's them know that there's someone out there who battled through health challenges just like they are and made it to the other side.

Feel free to leave a funny GIF in the comment section, as I've done that to nearly every status on this page.

Thanks, everyone!

And I should be leaving sometime today."

That one post took me two hours to complete. Reading it now, I still don't believe it's complete. I guess that's the struggle of being a writer.

I waited until the morning to finally post that on our Facebook page. A 2:00 AM post is never appropriate unless … actually, I don't have a joke this time. Time get it.

With the neck pain and being hooked up to wires, I barely got two hours of sleep that night.

Once it became 8:00 AM, a reasonable time to post on Facebook, I posted and got a ton of responses from wish grantors. Words can never describe how great my fellow wish grantors are.

That morning someone with Dr. Baehring's team came to my room and told me your scans didn't show any tumor growth. We don't have a diagnose for your pain.

My dad showed up the next morning and pleaded with me to start changing my life. "I want you to take better care of yourself. You need to put more time into your health."

He didn't directly say to forget about school and the book, but he pretty much implied more time needs to go away from that. When my dad is serious, he's serious. You do what he asks, and everything will be okay. If you fail to do what he asks, he'll continually hound you until you get it done. Which is what every great parent does.

I looked down and nodded my head. I didn't argue with him, as I knew he was right. I had put the school and book at the top of my list and forgot about my disabilities, which always need to take priority in my life. If I failed to take care of my disabilities, this process of ending up in the hospital will continually happen.

I took the post I wrote on Facebook and showed it to my mom. She thought it was a good post and posted it on her wall. It's always nice to have support.

Later that month my dad wanted me to go to a car show in New York City with him. I'm not a car person. When it comes to car shopping, all I ask for is a car that functions. That's all I need. I could care less about the brand or any of the fancy things that come with cars at car shows. I didn't want to go. But I realized how much my dad has been there for me my entire life. It would've been rude to say I won't go after all he's done for me. We left the next morning.

We drove to the car show and parked in a parking garage a few blocks from the show. Surprisingly it wasn't much of a struggle to walk that far, as when my body rests for a while it can handle a long walk. Being in the car for an hour allowed me to walk the few blocks to the Javits Center.

We walked into the building and bought tickets to one of the most famous car shows in the world. I didn't know that or care that much at the time. But my dad seemed to have the happiness I had on my wish trip, and the happiness I see on wish kids every time I grant a wish. I couldn't fight him.

What made the day a little better is that every time my dad spotted a chair, he told me to sit down, and he then looked at cars. I greatly appreciated his caring attitude.

The day of looking at random cars came to an end, and we walked out of the show.

With so much walking, I struggled to get to the car. The car was only eight blocks from the Javits Center, so thinking I was stronger than I truly was, I went for it.

After two blocks it felt like my legs were carrying 100 lbs. ankle weights. I didn't say anything to my dad, because I never admit defeat until I'm down.

We walked one more block, and as I pushed through, I knew my ankle would give out any second and then all of the sudden it happened. I was down.

Like a prize fighter getting knocked to the canvas, I fell on a New York City sidewalk. That's on the Mount Rushmore of worst places to fall. (Pardon My Take)

As I came crashing down, I knew it was over. Waiting to be helped up, I knew I had to organize my time better. The MFA program at Fairfield University couldn't be a part of my time anymore.

With that I went straight to my laptop and wrote an e-mail to Sonya, the program director, who had allowed me into her program"

"It's with a bittersweet feeling I have to say, I need to leave the MFA writing program. I wanted to wait till the last possible moment to finally admit it. That moment has finally come as registration for next semester is coming up. I thought maybe my health would turn positive over the past few months and maybe I could get to a point where I could find time for the program. It never occurred to me until the weekend I fell while walking around NYC. I simply have too much going on with my full-time job and worrying about my own physical health. Although I can't make it to the end of your program, I still want to thank all of you for helping me during my time in the program. People with disabilities often go to into a shell in fear, because they believe they can't do a certain task on their own. I know I've had moments where I turn the other way because of my disability. I still want to include my work from this program in my story. Although I didn't complete the program, my hope is that kids can read about my experience and fall in love with reading and writing at an earlier age.

This may sound silly, but I believe the program for me was like a second Make-A-Wish trip. My trip was to the MLB All-Star game because I wanted to see what it is like to be an MLB All-Star. My experience is the entire reason behind the memoir. Compared to your program, I wanted to see what it is like to be a writer. With the guest speakers and workshops, I've seen that. Before your program, I was looking on the internet for ghostwriters and getting nowhere. With no place to turn, I applied to the MFA program at Fairfield University, because I went to the high school on the Fairfield U campus. Also, my house was only five minutes away from campus. If I'm being honest, it was about location, too. I do believe it's entirely possible if I get rejected from the program I then think writing about my life is a dumb idea, I forget about writing the book and I move on with my life. That's why the MFA program is so important, even though I can't finish it. I'm content with the fact I made an attempt. That does mean a lot to me.

I thank all of you. My apologies if I missed other professors in the program who helped me." Every professor understood and wished me luck.

One good thing came from the Fairfield University writing program. I feel in love with reading. I went to the North Haven Library every two weeks and walked out with a new book. It felt like a crime to walk out of a place without paying for an item. This feeling came because I spent my entire life avoiding libraries. I found solace in playing video games and watching television. I laughed at the people who said 'the book was better than movie.' How could you say that? A book isn't projected on a screen and put in front of you. A movie requires minimal effort. In a movie, every scene is set up by the director for the viewer to enjoy. What's easier than that? A book requires a person to think, and who wants to do that? As I write this book, I've read over 150 memoirs over the past four years, and I must say, I get it. I can now see why people love reading. When you read a book, you get to be your own director. I spent 26 years of my life never reading, and I truly do regret that.

[]

28

Well, you made it to the last chapter of my book. Let me be the first to say—and the only one in this book to say,—I'm proud of you. Reading has become a lost art in our society as we spend our lives on Netflix binges or scrolling through Facebook liking photos of what our "friends" are doing.

My call is for you to be a reader. Me saying this isn't my way of taking down Silicon Valley. I've read over 150 books over the past four years. During those four years, I've scrolled through social media and watched Netflix too. All I'm asking for you to find time for reading. I've set up a rule for myself to read one new memoir every two weeks. There are some weeks I end up missing that rule. I just end up renewing the book and I keep reading until the end. Having that rule has changed my life, I spent my entire life doing my best to avoid reading. Please be a reader, I hope it'll change your life as much as it did for me. The power of a book is not an opportunity to miss out on.

To make this book happen, I sent this post to the private Make-A-Wish wish grantors Facebook page to help get it done"

"Hey everybody,

I hope you're all doing well during this trying time in our lives. I'm here to ask a favor. I'm still working on my book, and I'm at a dead end. Finding a publisher and editor is tough process. During this time, I've read around 150 books as a way of managing time away from writing the book, and I've grown to love reading. If you told me five years ago that I'd love to read, I would've laughed in your face. Reading and writing is one of the greatest art forms we have in our lives. At the end of every book, I always read the acknowledgments section. I read about how every writer had a whole group of people to thank. Believe it or not, no writer ever says that they did it on their own. I always assumed that writing was this all-encompassing task where one person sits at a desk and writes for a month and then you have a finished story. Writing is nothing like that. So, I'm here to ask for a favor. If anyone can help put me in contact with someone who I can trust to make a book possible, I would greatly appreciate it. Words couldn't even describe my feelings as this process has been long and difficult. Sometimes more difficult than my health history."

There is one tiny 'pro' that came out of this long process. I recently thought of the idea of creating a Make-A-Wish book club. My idea is that every single possible age, gender, and disease that's wish eligible needs to have a story from a wish kid. I know somewhere on this planet there is a 17-year-old boy with a brain tumor looking for someone to tell him it will be okay. He'd want to read about someone who already went through the exact same battle. That's why I wrote this book. If possible, I'd love to create a section on Amazon of just a ton of books from wish kids. If an eleven-year-old girl can read a book about someone her age who already battled cancer, think of how much easier her treatment will be.

Ideally, I think getting a large group of ghostwriters pooled together with each one having a specialty would be a great idea. It's just getting that group will be a challenge. Any thoughts and ideas would be greatly appreciated.

I've spent eight years on this book stressing every single word you've read. The doctor couldn't diagnose why I was getting severe head and neck pain during my latest hospital stay that I described in this book, but I'm sure that the reason I went to the hospital and I had to drop out of the writing program was because of the stress that came with writing this book. How many authors can say their book put them in the hospital? I worried that the average reader would pick this book up and give it a three-star review on the Internet. Could I handle that review? But in the end, this book is for one person and one person only. That person is me.

Before you think that's the most selfish thing you've ever heard, as much as this may seem like a joke, during my rehab from my spinal cord tumor, Jimmy Valmer the boy who uses crutches on South Park was the most relatable person I could find in 2004. A cartoon character from a television show was the only person I saw with a disability using crutches and still smiling. As silly as it sounds that gave me hope. I had no one else.

I wrote this book for myself, in the hope that the way I tell this story will help a child who's in the same situation I was in. I know that child is somewhere right now fearing what's next. As great as Jimmy Valmer is, that character didn't allow me to see what's next. He's remained the same age since 2004. I'm allowing kids to see 17 more years of life with a lot of ups and downs throughout. I hope this book can be a guide for sick children everywhere. Learn from my mistakes. I did put some positives into this story when it came to living with my disability to show that even though you have a disability you can do good. I know that on November 19, 2004, I would've wished for a book just like this one.

At this point you may be asking, 'Cory, do you wish your life were different?' I honestly don't. I'm sure if you interviewed me the day before my mom saw my spine was curved and asked, 'Cory, what do you want from life?' I would've said, "To be healthy and very normal."

Instead, today I'm living with a brain tumor, spinal cord tumor, Crohn's disease, and a far from normal life. You saw that none of this has been normal. I actually have three diseases that are eligible for a wish from Make-A-Wish.

The reason I wouldn't change anything is because I believe in the Butterfly Effect. Meaning if you take one part away from this story, the rest of the story won't be the same. Sure, my high school experience at Fairfield Prep was nothing like a typical high school student because of my disability, but it was a teacher at Fairfield Prep who got me into the Foundation. If I went to a different school, do I get into the Foundation? We will never know. Thank you, Ms. Laguzza. If I never attend Fairfield University, do I give up on this book and never attempt to write it? Again, I don't know. Thank you, Sonya Huber and Elizabeth Hastings, for accepting me into the program and giving me a chance. That's all people with disabilities want—just a chance. As much as you can try to turn my life into a puzzle and create new puzzle pieces to see how this book would end, you simply can't. It played out the way it played out.

In the end, there's truly one variable I guarantee you can't take out of the story for a different result. That's me getting sick and being brought into to the greatest charity on the planet. I remember who I was before Cathie and Georgianna came to visit me and told me about Make-A-Wish. I'm not saying I was a bad kid before I got sick; I was just a kid who watched ESPN and the "My Wish" segments every summer and thought that it was cool what they're doing for sick children. I never thought about volunteering. Once Make-A-Wish helped me, I knew I had to come back and help them. I've loved every minute of it. This Foundation has created great purpose in my life, and for that I will be forever grateful.

It happens every morning where I'm reminded of how my teenage years were scraped away from me. I lift my shirt up before entering the shower and stare at a body I've grown to despise. At 30, I hover around 120 pounds as eating a meal is a major struggle for me. When your spine is curved and you suffer from Crohn's disease, every meal is a new challenge. I look at my body as my ribs jettison out. Below that, I see a hole where my feeding tube used to be. Fun times.

Next is a scar from my brain shunt placement; without that brain shunt, who knows if I'm still alive writing this book. That's just another variable on the long list of variables. And finally, where this story began, I turn to my side and look at my back. I look at a back with kyphosis that bends at an 80-degree angle and a spine that curves at a 45-degree angle because of scoliosis. If any of my abnormal body parts deserves a lifetime achievement award, it's my back.

After everything you've read in this book, I can be honest to tell you that I'm also a little bitter and none of this should have happened to me. My life could've been so much different if none of this happened. The social struggles started with that story of me dancing with that girl in eighth grade. That was the start of my downfall when it came to confidence in myself. That's why I told that story and some of the other sadder and lonely stories you read in this book. I didn't like the person I had become because of these tumor cells. For all the happiness and good things that were accomplished in this book, don't make the social mistakes I made. I pointed those mistakes out so you don't become me in that way. Sure, follow my lead in terms of caring about other wish kids. But don't think because you're disabled that you are any worse off than anyone else. If anything, it gives you a story to publish in a book. And that's something to take pride in. I wish I knew that on November 19, 2004.

I'll be the first to admit I have my own set of faults. I have an unhealthy addiction to fantasy football, and I play too many video games. We all have our vices that take away from the important things in life. I'm not telling you to change your life and never do any of the fun things you love to do. All I ask is that you use your gift of life and take some time out of the day to care about the Make-A-Wish Foundation.

The first thing you can do is to tell others about this book and the Make-A-Foundation. I want the whole world to know and understand what the Foundation is about. Knowledge is power. (Family Guy)

Finally, I'll just say this to the child who's just like me, "DON'T LET YOUR DISABILITY DEFEAT YOU." You can forget every story you read in this book. I wouldn't be offended by that. This book is 81,832 words. I'm sure you have a lot going on in your life and you forgot most of it. I just need you to remember that one sentence. You saw throughout these pages that socially, I let my tumor cells beat me. I'd love to know how my life would've turned out if these tumor cells never entered by body. How would a healthy Cory Metz have lived his life? Would I have been social butterfly? Going to parties and attending different schools as I didn't have to worry about my health? If there was a mirror where I could watch how my life turned out as a perfectly healthy teenager, I would be lying if I said I wouldn't be a little interested. But in this hypothetical situation, would that mean I never know and work with the Make-A-Wish Foundation? Sure, it would be great to be the guy who is the life of the party. The guy who's had steady relationships and friendships. There are so many things I have missed out on because of one MRI scan. But the true reason I wouldn't look in the mirror and take that life of the perfectly healthy me is because of the Make-A-Wish Foundation. If this story was just me telling you about how I failed to live in society after being diagnosed with a disability, the book still would've explained what it's like to live with a disability, but you don't get the satisfaction of knowing I'm happier with my life because of the power of the Make-A-Wish Foundation. Without the Foundation, this book truly has no greater purpose. For that I will be forever grateful.

Well, that's it. I hope you enjoyed my story and do your best in life to be a reader. Wait, this is it, I swear. Another reason I have to let go of this book is because I'm currently in talks with Mass General about radiation treatment. I need to focus on that and let this book go. This book has been a drawn-out process because I fear I didn't do enough. What if a wish kid has more questions that I didn't answer in this book? So, I've done my best to solve that issue. My e-mail is iamnotgordon91@gmail.com. I had to end this book with one more joke by having a funny e-mail. If you have any questions or comments, please e-mail me. Or you just want a friend to talk with. Thank you. And who knows, maybe we will have a sequel to this book where I discuss my possible treatment and life after this book. Cliffhanger........................ (The Dan LeBatard Show and Anchorman)

100% of the profits from this book go to Make-A-Wish Connecticut. That leaves me with one question even though I know the answer, "did you give?" (I Think You Should Leave with Tim Robinson)

Acknowledgements

First let me say thank you to Richard Gelfand. I walked away from this book multiple times over the years, and I always found it tough to come back. The final time I came back to writing the book, I had a partner in Richard, and we got to the end. I'll be forever grateful.

Second the beautiful cover art for this book was completed by Diana Nuhn. This book is truly complete because of her work. Thank you.

In terms of the important people throughout my life, the ones I need to thank first are the three other members of my family. First is my mother. Without her I don't know where my life would be. She never took a moment off from caring for me, and she always stayed by my side whenever I was scared.

Second is my dad. What's there to say? My brother and I call my dad 'the big guy.' In the movie Wedding Crashers, Owen Wilson says, "There he is, it's the big guy." Watch that part of the movie; the way Owen Wilson is so happy, and he just yells that line. That sums up the way I feel about being around my dad. Thanks for always being there, big guy.

Last, but not least in my family is my brother. 'Hey brother.' (Arrested Development) When you have a best friend with you since birth, it makes your life that much easier. Thanks for the memories we've shared and everything we've done together over the years.

Next on my list of people to thank has to be Ms. Laguzza, who started this entire story with Make-A-Wish. If she never speaks up for me and helps me get into the Make-A-Wish Foundation, then none of this is possible.

To my wish grantors, Georgianna Hull and Cathie Allen, thank you. If you two aren't the caring individuals you are, and for my money, the best wish grantors in the Foundation, I don't know if I would have cared enough to come back into the Foundation. Thank you.

To the wish families I've worked with, it was an honor to help with your wishes. Together we did amazing work, and I hope we've inspired a few new volunteers by describing what we accomplished together.

To the wish grantors I've worked with, thanks for helping me along the way. We are truly doing something that is life-changing on a daily basis. That's something that's hard to accomplish.

To the Make-A-Wish Connecticut chapter, you took in a teenager who was at his lowest, and you built the person who does all of this work in your Foundation. It all started with Cheryl Bieling answering my e-mail and allowing me back into the Foundation. Again, I don't know what my life is without the Foundation. It's nothing I want to discover. And a thank you to Pam Keough, who's the President and CEO of Make-A-Wish Connecticut. She runs the whole show in the Connecticut chapter, and her guidance makes the chapter work so well. To all the staff I've met and known at the Connecticut chapter, thank you! The Make-A-Wish organization gives me purpose in life, and no words can truly describe that.

To my boss, Dorothy Siniscalchi, thank you for granting me a job when I was at my lowest and searching for something. And thanks to all of my co-workers at IUOE Local 478. You've asked about this book, and I kept saying eventually it'll be done. We finally got to eventually.

I feel like this a speech at the Oscars where the winner goes, "I know I'm forgetting someone." Instead, I'm not getting 'played off'—I just have a terrible memory. I don't know if you're reading this book just know I consider you a friend and I thank you.

Made in United States
North Haven, CT
29 March 2022

17657000R00192